# Think Through History

# Changing Minds

## Britain 1500-1750

**Authors:**

**Jamie Byrom**

**Christine Counsell**

**Michael Riley**

**Paul Stephens-Wood**

 LONGMAN

# Changing Minds – Britain 1500 to 1750

## Introduction

## Your enquiries

### Life and death

Henry VII 1485-1509    Henry VIII 1509-1547    Edward VI 1547-1553    Mary I 1553-1558    Elizabeth I 1558-1603    James I 1603-1625

**1534** Act of Supremacy
**1536** Execution of William Tyndale
**1536** Dissolution of monasteries begins

**1559** Elizabethan religious settlement
**1587** Execution of Mary, Queen of Scots
**1588** The Spanish Armada

**1601** Poor Law introduced
**1605** The Gunpowder Plot

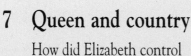

Charles I 1625-1649    The Republic 1649-1660    Charles II 1660-1685    James II 1685-1688    William & Mary 1688-1702    Anne 1702-1714    George I 1714-1727    George II 1727-1760

o Pilgrim Fathers sail to America

1642 Civil War begins

1649 Charles I executed

1658 Death of Oliver Cromwell

1660 Monarchy restored

1666 The Great Fire of London

1685 Monmouth's Rebellion

1688 The Glorious Revolution

1707 England and Scotland united

1721 Robert Walpole became Britain's 'First Prime Minister'

1745 Jacobite rebellion

# Introduction
## Changing Minds

The picture above shows a shocking event. On a bitterly cold day in January 1649 an axe cut through the neck of King Charles I, ruler of England, Scotland, Ireland and Wales. The executioner held up the head and showed it to the crowd. People had **changed their minds about how they should be ruled**. They never again allowed their **monarchs** to have so much power.

The man in this picture is about to be
burnt alive. His name is William Tyndale.
He was **executed** in 1536 because he
translated the Bible from Latin into
English so that ordinary people could read
it. In the sixteenth century many people
**changed their minds about
religion**. The Church changed and so
did people's beliefs.

In 1589 the three women in this picture were hanged by
their necks until they choked to death. In the sixteenth and
seventeenth centuries thousands of women were hanged or
burnt because people thought that they were witches.

In the eighteenth century this stopped. Many people were
beginning to **change their minds about how
the world worked**. They began to look for natural
and scientific reasons to explain why things happened.

The enquiries in this book are about the **changing
minds** of people who lived in Britain between 1500
and 1750. These people are dead and gone, but if we ask good,
thoughtful questions we can begin to understand their world.

# Dead and gone

## How can we learn about hidden lives?

*The Tichborne Dole, 1670*

This is a famous picture from the seventeenth century. At the front is Sir Henry Tichborne. He is standing with his family and friends. These people are the gentry. They are rich and powerful landowners. Hidden in the background you can see the ordinary people. Some of them are Sir Henry's servants. Others live in his village and rent their land from him. The picture shows Sir Henry giving out bread to the poor people of the village.

## Think

- Describe Sir Henry Tichborne.
- Describe the gentry.
- Describe the servants and villagers.

We usually divide people who lived between 1500 and 1750 into three main groups.

# The Gentry

Some **gentry** were great nobles who spent most of their time at **court** with the monarch. Others, like Sir Henry Tichborne, did not go to court but were the most important people in their counties.

# The Middling Sort

Some of the **middling sort** were merchants and master-craftsmen who worked in the towns. But very few people lived in towns compared to today. Most of the middling sort were yeoman farmers who owned or rented some land.

# The Lower Sort

The **lower sort** had no land. They worked as servants and labourers on farms or in towns. If they could not find work they often became beggars.

## Think

- Which groups of people do you think it is most difficult for historians to find out about? Why?

# Your enquiry

It is quite easy to find out about the gentry. They built wonderful houses which we can still visit today. They often wrote letters and kept diaries. Their faces still stare at us from their portraits. Finding out about the middling and lower sorts is more difficult. They have not left as much evidence. Their lives are hidden from us. But if we ask clever questions we can discover a lot. In this enquiry you will ask lots of **big questions** and little questions to find out about the lives of ordinary people.

# At home

One way to find out about people in the past is to look at their houses. The houses of the lower sort have mostly fallen down, but many of the houses which were built by the middling sort of people are still lived in today. The house in the picture below belonged to a **yeoman** farmer. Many new houses like this were built in the seventeenth century. Their owners were very proud of the new glass windows, chimneys and extra rooms.

*A photograph of a yeoman's house in the village of Abernodwydd, Wales*

The photograph below shows what the inside of a yeoman's house might have looked like in the seventeenth century.

We can find out a lot more about people's houses from **inventories**. These are lists of things which people owned. Most inventories were made when middling sorts of people died so that their property could be shared out fairly among their family and friends. The inventory on the next page lists the things which a man called John Every owned when he died in 1668.

*A reconstruction of the inside of a yeoman's house in Abernodwydd*

8

## A true inventory of the goods and chattels of John Every

In the hall
One table, one form, one cupboard. His clothes.
In a chamber over the hall
Two beds, five chests, one box.
In the kitchen
One spit, four hooks, one cheesewring, three brass pots, three brass pans, one kettle.
In the kitchen chamber
One little bed, one wimsheet.
In a little buttery
Two barrels, one tub, one silter.
Other goods
Apples Cheese Two cows An old horse Two pigs

### Strange words

*chattels* – possessions
*cheesewring* – used for making cheese
*form* – a bench
*silter* – a tub for salting meat
*wimsheet* – used for separating grain

Historians have studied thousands of inventories from the period 1500–1750. They have reached some interesting conclusions.

## Conclusion 1

Middling sorts of people usually lived in houses with more than six rooms. Many of them built bigger and better houses in the years between 1570 and 1640. The lower sort of people usually lived in houses with two or three rooms.

## Conclusion 2

Many people earnt a living by farming as well as following a trade or craft. Some middling people owned big farms. Others made a lot of money as **merchants**.

## Conclusion 3

Life was becoming much more comfortable over the period 1500–1750. Many people began to own things like pewter plates, linen sheets and comfortable chairs.

## Think

- How many rooms were there in John Every's house?
- What do you think each room was used for?
- How do you think John Every made a living?

## STEP 1

Historians find out about the past by asking questions. Lots of questions about the past are interesting, but some are **bigger** than others. Sort these questions into **big questions** and little questions and copy them onto a table like the one below. Two of the questions have already been sorted for you. (Don't try to answer the questions – just **sort** them!)

### Inventories

| Big questions | Little questions |
|---|---|
| How hygienic were people in sixteenth-century Britain? | Did John Every have a toilet in his house? |

How did people cook their food in the seventeenth century?
What was a silter?
Did John Every wear underpants?
How hygienic were people in sixteenth-century Britain?
What work did people do?
Did John Every have a toilet in his house?
Did life get better for ordinary people between 1500 and 1750?
How much did a pig cost in 1683?

# The facts of life

This picture shows Lord Cobham and his family in 1567. The fine clothes and food show you that this was a gentry family.

It is quite easy to find out about the family life of the gentry. They have left portraits, diaries, letters and other **sources**. It is much harder to find out about the families of the middling and lower sorts of people. However, even these people have left some clues behind them. From 1538 all priests had to keep a record of the **baptisms**, marriages and burials in their **parishes**. Nearly everyone went to church at that time so the parish **registers** record almost all the baptisms, marriages and deaths which happened. These are some entries from the parish register of Easingwold in Yorkshire in the summer of 1650:

Robert, the son of Edward Bell was baptised, May 12

Alice, the daughter of Robert Raynold was baptised, May 26

William, the son of Francis Driffield was baptised, June 6

William, the above-named son of Francis Driffield was buried, June 7

Isabell Hogson, a lame and poor widow was buried, June 13

Richard, the son of George Cundall, was baptised July 7

Michael Pearson was buried, July 10

Thomas Johnson and Anne Cuthbert both of this parish were married, July 30

Joanne Raper, an old woman was buried, August 13

A child of William Goodrick the younger died unbaptised and was buried, September 1

*Parish register of Easingwold in Yorkshire, 1650*

## Think

- How can you tell that William Driffield was a baby when he died?

- What clues does the parish register give us about why Isabell Hogson was poor?

Historians have put together the information about baptisms, marriages and burials from hundreds of parish registers. They have reached some interesting **conclusions**:

## Conclusion 1

About one in five babies died before their first birthday.

## Conclusion 2

Nearly a third of all children did not reach the age of ten.

## Conclusion 3

People usually got married in their mid-twenties.

## Conclusion 4

Many people moved away from the village where they were born.

## Conclusion 5

Many women were pregnant when they got married.

## Conclusion 6

There were major outbreaks of **plague** in 1563, 1593 and 1695.

## Conclusion 7

Over the period 1550–1750 the **population** of England doubled.

**STEP 2**

When historians use parish registers, they find themselves asking both **big** and little questions. Copy this table and add some **big** and little questions of your own.

### Parish Registers

| Big questions | Little questions |
|---|---|
| Did the population increase between 1550 and 1750? | How many people were married in Easingwold in 1650? |
| How old were people when they married? | How old was William Driffield when he died? |

# Behaving badly

During the period 1500 to 1750, the law was still very harsh. Nowadays criminals are fined or sent to prison. In the seventeenth century people could be hanged for a small crime like stealing a sheep.

There was no police force, but in every village constables and **churchwardens** made sure that people who broke the law were brought to trial. Details of court cases were written down by clerks. Here are two examples:

> William Yewill, labourer, for stealing corn worth 10d. from Richard Brothwood. Found guilty. To be whipped.

> Anthony Bray, yeoman, and his wife Magdalen, for pretending they were robbed by Turkish pirates. She found guilty. To be branded with the letter 'C' on her forehead.

*Bedfordshire Quarter Sessions Records, 1659*

Historians have used records like these to piece together the lives of different criminals. These are the crimes of Henry Abbot, a yeoman from Earls Colne in Cumbria:

- Fighting with William Clark and breaking his finger
- Leaving his house in the middle of the night wearing only his shirt
- Playing cards, dice and other games
- Swearing at his neighbours
- Refusing to clean out his ditch
- Cutting down trees without permission
- Being drunk

**STEP 3**

**Copy out and continue this table with big questions and little questions about crime.**

<u>Criminal Records</u>

| Big questions | Little questions |
| --- | --- |
| Which crimes were most common in the sixteenth century? | Why did Anthony Bray pretend to be robbed by Turkish pirates? |

# Thinking your enquiry through

You are now going to make a diagram to show how we can find out about the hidden lives of ordinary people.

On a very large sheet of paper draw the circles like this. You will need to make them much bigger than the ones here.

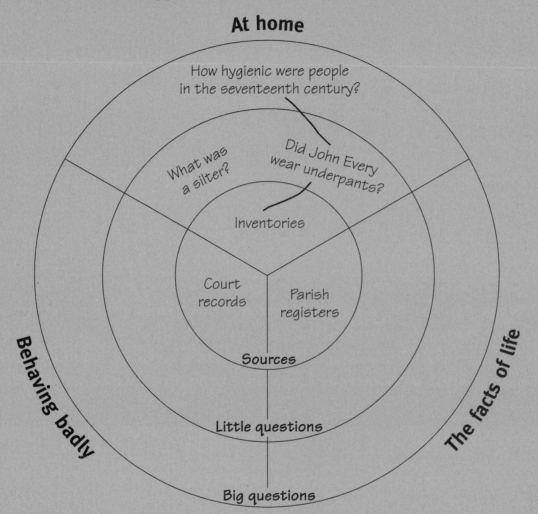

1 In the centre write all the types of sources you have used in this enquiry.

2 In the second circle write your little questions.

3 In the third circle write your big questions.

4 When you have included as many sources and questions as you can, turn your diagram into an enquiry web to show links between little questions, big questions and sources. Two of the links have been done for you. Finish the web by making more links of your own.

# 'So famous a city' ②

## What was fine and what was foul in London life?

This picture was made soon after 1600. It shows the River Thames near the Tower of London. You can see some fine, trading ships on the river. Ships such as these brought goods from all over Europe to London. London was one of Europe's largest and most famous cities. The written source shows what one German visitor thought about London in 1592.

*Detail from Visscher's Panorama, seventeenth century*

London is a large, excellent and mighty city of business. Most of the **inhabitants** are employed in buying and selling and trading with almost every corner of the world. The river is most useful for this purpose. Ships from many kingdoms come almost up to the city. They bring goods in and take away others in exchange.

It is a very crowded city. One can scarcely pass along the streets on account of the throng. The people are extremely proud. They care little for foreigners. They scoff and laugh at them. One dare not oppose these Londoners else the street boys gather and strike. We have to put up with insult as well as injury.

## Think

● What does the German visitor admire about London?

● What does the German visitor dislike about London?

14

## Your enquiry

It is the year 1606. London is as busy as ever and it is still growing. As its size has increased so have its problems. One English writer has complained that many things now 'blemish so famous a city' – but life goes on.

In this enquiry you take the role of a young trader from Italy. You and your brother have just arrived in London on a ship like one of those in the picture. An English friend is going to show you around London. What will delight you – and what will disgust you?

# From ship to shore

It is early morning. You and your brother are on the deck of your ship. You have heard about England and how it rains all the time. When your ship arrived it was raining heavily. Now as you look down at the river, it is brown with mud.

Your ship is not alone. There are dozens of tall-masted sailing ships unloading goods from all over the world. Other ports have fine docks but in London the largest ships such as yours have to drop anchor in the middle of the river. You have been to many great ports – but London is the busiest of all.

## Think

- Why do you think some ships have to stay in the middle of the river?
- Which languages might you have heard spoken as the ships were unloaded?

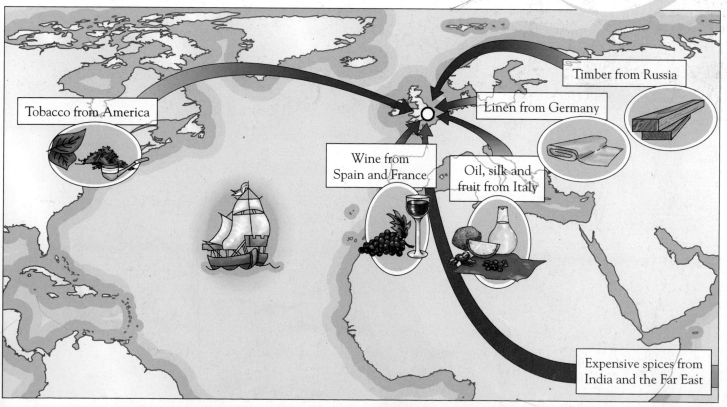

Tobacco from America

Wine from Spain and France

Oil, silk and fruit from Italy

Linen from Germany

Timber from Russia

Expensive spices from India and the Far East

*Some of London's main trading links in 1606*

Soon you are on a small boat which is taking you ashore. The weather is so cold compared with Italy. As your men row hard against the current, your brother points towards the city. It is full of church spires and tightly-packed houses.

You see the famous Tower of London. Your father has told you all about this mighty castle. Behind its strong walls are the king's jewels, his supplies of weapons and a remarkable collection of wild animals from all over the world.

Then you hear a loud noise. Up ahead you see what look like rapids in the river! The water is flowing so powerfully under the twenty famous arches of London Bridge that it looks like series of small waterfalls. A few brave and skilful men steer their small boats towards you, downstream, through the arches of the bridge. Your own boat is heading for the south bank of the river just by the bridge. As it nears the bank you see your friend waiting for you.

He greets you and your brother warmly and leads you up some steps to the gates which open onto London Bridge. Above you is a gruesome sight: skulls of **traitors** are fixed on wooden poles high over the gates for all to see. This is how the English remind their people to obey the king. What a welcome to London!

## Think

- Why were skulls put up above the gates on London Bridge?

- Which things mentioned on pages 15 and 16 can you find in the picture below?

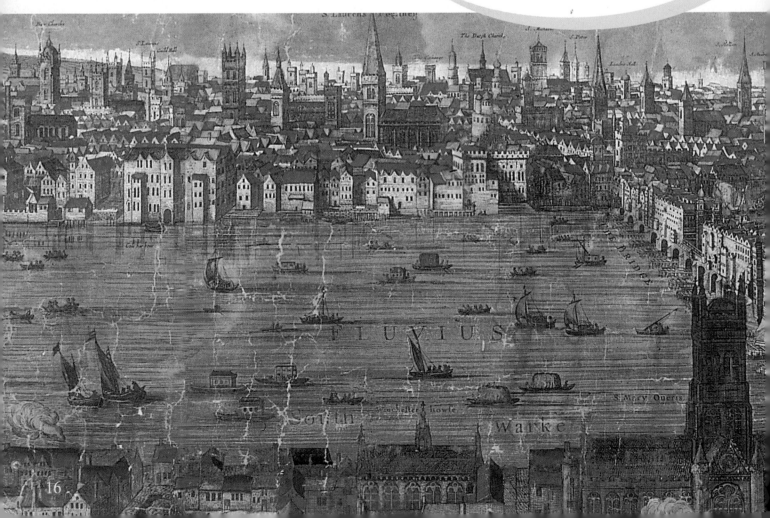

You cross the bridge. It feels as if you are passing through a long tunnel because houses have been built on either side of the road. The top floors of the houses are joined so it is dark down at street level. Every so often there is a gap between the houses and you can see the muddy waters rushing past below. All sorts of rubbish are floating downstream, including human waste and rotting vegetables.

Soon you reach the end of the bridge. Here it is – the famous city of London.

**STEP 1**

**Work in pairs. Each of you is to be one of the Italian brothers. One brother is an optimist. An optimist is a person who looks on the bright side of life and always finds good things to enjoy. The other brother is a pessimist. A pessimist always takes a gloomy view and only seems to notice problems.**

**Look through the section called 'From ship to shore' and make a list of things you have noticed about London. Remember the optimist will list the good points about London. The pessimist will list the bad points.**

*Detail from Visscher's Panorama, seventeenth century, showing the River Thames near London Bridge*

# Delights and dangers

All around you people are noisily taking down the
shutters from their windows and setting up shop stalls.
Most streets are narrow and winding. A flock of sheep
is herded past you. They bleat noisily and scramble
their way along the mud-filled lane. They are
brought in alive so that the meat is fresh when
the butchers sell it.

London is busy and exciting – but it is very messy too.
Heavy wagons rumble past, swaying dangerously. Mud
splashes onto your clothes. It makes a foul smell.
You soon see why. You pass a butcher who is hacking
open the carcass of a cow and throwing all the unwanted
offal into the centre of the street. Crows drop from the
sky to take what they can, but there is still a large
pile of waste. Worst of all, chamber pots are being
emptied from windows high above you.

The waste is blocking the open drain
which runs down the centre of the street.
A trickle is running through. It is a
mixture of rainwater, animal blood and
urine. Your friend says the air is often
poisoned by this filth. He is sure it
causes plague.

You pass a large water tank. This water is piped up
from the River Thames for people to take to their homes.
A water-seller is collecting water in leather bags. He takes
a heavy club from his belt and swings it around his head to
clear the crowds away from the tank. You move on quickly.

Soon you arrive at the Royal Exchange. This is the centre of London's trade. Your friend swells with pride as he takes you inside. Around a stone-paved courtyard merchants are meeting and agreeing prices for their goods. Shops sell gold, books, glass, armour, and even mousetraps and birdcages. Your own cargo of oils and herbs from Italy will soon be on sale here.

By now you are quite tired so your English friend leads you north towards the famous city walls near Bishopsgate. The air is fresher here. You walk through the open fields to the north of the city. This is where Londoners go to relax.

## Think

- What signs are there on the map that the countryside begins just outside the city walls?

- What signs are there on the map that the city has started to spread outside its walls?

*Part of the Agas map, made in 1560*

The fresh air restores your strength and you turn back into the city at Cripplegate. After passing through more muddy streets you reach Cheapside. This is a wide street filled with stalls showing a huge range of goods. Among the crowds street traders are calling out to attract customers. You also hear a 'Crier' bellowing out news to the people. What a city this is!

STEP 2

Go back through the section called 'Delights and dangers'. Add more ideas to the list you started in Step 1. Remember! The optimist looks on the bright side. The pessimist sees plenty to grumble about.

19

# Into the pit

Your friend has a surprise for you. It is a dry day so the open-air theatres on the south bank of the river will be putting on plays. There is to be a new play by William Shakespeare at the Globe Theatre. This is exciting news. People in Italy have heard how fine the English theatre is.

From Cheapside you walk to the banks of the River Thames. You are quickly surrounded by several noisy and dirty watermen offering to row you across the river. Before long you are in midstream wondering whether you will get across safely.

When you reach the south bank your friend pays the waterman. He tells you that the watermen love to charge foreigners more than they should. Of course, some foreigners in London are not really foreigners any more. People from all over Europe have run away to England to start a new life because of wars over religion in their own countries.

## Think

- Why did so many foreigners come to London in the seventeenth century?

- Why were some foreigners in London not really foreigners any more?

Your brother points out a flag that is flying high above the theatre. This means a play will soon begin. You join a crowd heading towards the theatre entrance. Your English friend advises you to hold tightly onto the purse that hangs from your belt. **Cutpurses** mingle in these crowds and they can slice off a purse without you feeling a thing.

Some of the crowd turn away towards another theatre. You start to follow them but your friend calls you back. He explains that they are going to watch the **bear baiting**. Bear baiting is where a bear is chained to a post while hounds leap at it, drawing blood with their sharp teeth. Sometimes the target is a bull who tosses the dogs high with his horns.

*A Tudor print showing bear and bull baiting*

Finally you reach the theatre. You pay to sit high in a gallery. Down below the poorest people are standing by the stage. The area they are standing in is called the pit. They look a pretty rough lot, but the people sitting near you are well-dressed and polite.

The play begins. It is called 'Macbeth'. There are moments of great poetry and moments of great comedy. There is much cheering and jeering at the actors – especially at the women, who are played by young boys. Everyone feels a strange thrill when witches or ghosts appear on stage. There is a battle scene near the end when animal blood is splashed all over those nearest the stage!

As you leave the theatre a fight breaks out. It grows into a small riot and your friend hurries you away. He explains that this often happens when large crowds gather and there is too much drinking. Strict church-goers, called **Puritans**, want the theatre to be banned.

You cross the river again and your friend points to the west. He says he will take you past the bend in the river tomorrow to see the king's palace and the rich men's houses near Westminster. Today there is just one more place to visit – for the best view in the whole city.

*This is a photograph of a modern audience enjoying a play at the new Globe Theatre. The Globe was a Tudor theatre in London. It has recently been rebuilt to look as much like the original Tudor theatre as possible.*

## Think

- Why do you think that the theatre was so popular in Tudor times?

- Why do you think that the Puritans thought theatres and plays were wicked?

## STEP 3

Go back through the section called 'Into the pit' and add more information to the list you started in Step 1.

# Panorama

Your friend leads you back up from the river to St Paul's Church. A crowd is breaking up as you arrive. These are Puritans who have spent the past two hours listening to a sermon by a preacher outside the church.

You work your way through the crowd and enter the church. It is just like a market place. All sorts of traders are packing away their goods. Fishmongers are even clearing away fish from the tombs which have been used as a shop counter.

You make your way up a dark staircase and finally appear in the open air at the top of the church tower. From here you can see the whole city. Down below you, people are closing the shutters on their houses. Some have fixed burning torches to their walls to guide people as the streets grow dark. You look at the tightly-packed timber houses with their top floors overhanging the street. Surely there is a terrible danger of fire? Your friend tells you not to worry. He leads you down the steps and across the street to an inn. Your long day is drawing to a close.

*Detail from Visscher's Panorama, seventeenth century, showing the River Thames, the Globe Theatre and St Paul's Church*

Go back through the section called 'Panorama' and add new information to the list you started in Step 1.

# Thinking your enquiry through

The source at the start of this enquiry showed what one foreign visitor thought about London. He realised that in some ways it was fine but in other ways it was foul. Unfortunately, the Italian brothers in our enquiry cannot see both points of view! Look at the cartoon. The two brothers are inside a London inn. They have begun to argue. One brother is convinced that London is a wonderful city. The other brother hates it.

Act out their disagreement in a role play. Work in the pairs you chose in Step 1. Each of you takes the role of one of the brothers. One is the optimist. The other is the pessimist. You must try to persuade your brother that you are right about London and that he is wrong. Use as many examples as you can from the lists you made in Steps 1, 2, 3 and 4.

Here are some of the things which you are sure to disagree about!

**The River Thames**
**Buildings**
**Streets**
**Trade**
**Noise**
**Crowds**
**The treatment of foreigners**
**Entertainment**
**Safety**

# Vagrants and vagabonds

## Did life change for the beggars of Bristol?

*A soap-eater, sixteenth century*

Imagine taking some soap and chewing it until your mouth is frothing and bubbling and you look as if you have a terrible disease. It would be very unpleasant and no one should try it – but you would probably recover.

Now imagine something far, far worse. Imagine deliberately breaking your ankle and twisting it until it has no chance of mending properly. You would think that nothing could make a person do something so desperate. You would be wrong.

Hunger can make people do awful things. These two pictures are from England in the sixteenth century. The man above is a soap-eater. He tries to get people to give him money by looking terribly ill. The man below cannot walk properly. We do not know if this particular beggar deliberately injured himself, but some did.

Beggars at this time knew that the law would **help** them if they were disabled. They also knew that the law **punished** beggars who were fit and healthy.

*A cripple, sixteenth century*

Wandering beggars who appeared to be healthy were punished cruelly. They were called **vagrants** or **vagabonds**. This source was written in 1586. It describes the harsh laws for vagabonds:

If he is judged to be a vagabond, he is to be whipped and a hole burnt in the lobe of his ear with a hot iron. If he is found guilty again, his other ear will be burnt and he will be made a servant. If he is found guilty a third time, he will be condemned to death.

*William Harrison, from 'The Description of England' 1586*

## Think

- Why do you think that the government made these harsh laws?

- Do you think that punishments like these would have stopped people from becoming vagabonds?

In the sixteenth century there were more and more laws about the treatment of poor people. These laws show us that rich and powerful people were getting very worried. The number of poor people seemed to be growing. All over the country the richer people tried to solve the problem. But no matter what they did, the problem would not go away.

## Your enquiry

**In this enquiry you will study just one city – Bristol. You will examine what the rich people did about the problem of the poor. During the sixteenth and seventeenth centuries the powerful people who ran the city of Bristol kept on trying new solutions. But did they really change anything? At the end of the enquiry you will reach your own conclusion about how much changed and how much stayed the same in the treatment of Bristol's poor.**

# An old problem grows

In 1601 the most powerful men in the city of Bristol were called together by the **mayor**. They were going to spend yet another meeting trying to work out what to do with the poorest people of the city.

These wealthy men were called **burgesses**. Some of the burgesses must have felt like giving up. They had been trying to sort this out for more than sixty years. But the problem had been getting worse, not better.

The burgesses probably had different ideas about why the number of poor people was growing all the time.

We can imagine what they might have said:

I think that King Henry VII started the problem when he stopped barons from having private armies. It stopped rebellions, but it took work away from thousands!

It was worst in the 1590s I think. The weather kept ruining the harvest. Food was scarce and prices went up and up. The poorest always suffer most when that happens, don't they?

No. The worst problems came when Henry VIII shut down the monasteries in 1536. They used to care for the poor ... now we have to do it!

Nonsense! There is plenty of work about. Most of these vagrants are just too lazy to work. We have never been tough enough on them.

It's the land-owners' fault. Too many people have started to keep sheep instead of growing crops. They get a good price for the wool but they don't need so many workers.

Yes, many of these people are wicked **rogues**. They come to our fine town because they want to steal our goods and riches.

## Think

- List the different types of people whom the burgesses blamed.

What really upset the burgesses was that so many poor people were breaking the rules. People were supposed to stay in their parish. In fact, thousands were becoming vagabonds. They were wandering from place to place ... and too many were coming to Bristol.

*A sixteenth-century print showing a vagabond family on the move*

The burgesses must have been angry. Bristol was a proud city. It was the most important port in England after London. Over 10,000 people lived within its old **medieval** walls. For years it had done its best to look after its poor. Rich merchants built **almshouses** for the needy. When the harvest failed in the 1590s they brought in grain from Europe. In 1596 the burgesses gave a free meal of meat every day until the famine passed. Most burgesses did not mind looking after the poor people of Bristol, but why should they look after outsiders?

## Think

- Why do you think that the burgesses helped the poor people so much during the famines of the 1590s?

- Why might the burgesses have been scared of the poor?

What made the problem even worse was that there were so many different types of poor people. It was hard to sort them all out.

● **Some** had lived in Bristol for years ... **others** were new arrivals.

● **Some** were ill but would recover ... **others** were too old or lame to work again.

● **Some** were fit and seemed keen to find work ... **others** were fit and able but preferred to beg, steal or pretend to be injured.

The burgesses thought that the able-bodied vagrants were the worst of all. Some formed large gangs and spoke to each other in their own strange language as they threatened or robbed the people they met.

The law already allowed the city authorities to punish some poor people very harshly. The 1572 Poor Law had said that vagrants and vagabonds must be whipped and have a large hole bored through the flap of one ear with a red hot iron at least an inch wide. These punishments were used in Bristol, but were they punishing the right people? Many burgesses were not sure. And why did the problem not go away?

## STEP 1

**Write a heading: The sixteenth century. Use everything you have read so far in this enquiry to make two lists:**

1 How some of the poor in Bristol were helped

2 How some of the poor in Bristol were punished

# A new law arrives

## The 1601 Poor Law

At their meeting in February 1601 the mayor of Bristol showed the burgesses an important document. It was a new law from Parliament, bearing Queen Elizabeth's royal seal. This law was to be used all over the country. The burgesses would have to make it work in Bristol. They read it carefully.

The churchwardens of every parish shall ...

... set to work all persons who have no daily trade to get their living

... raise weekly, by taxation of richer people of the parish, sums of money to provide wool, thread and iron to set the poor to work

... pay money towards the relief of any lame, old, blind or other poor who are not able to work

... make the children of some poor live with local craftsmen and learn a trade as apprentices

... send to a **gaol** or a **house of correction** any who refuse to work

... whip until bloody any vagabond out of his parish and send him back to his home

The Justice of the Peace must make sure that this law is carried out properly.

*Extracts from the 1601 Poor Law*

## Think

● List all the ways in which this law tried to make poor people work.

● What do you think that rich people would have thought about this law? (Read it again, carefully.)

The mayor and the burgesses of Bristol could see that this law was not completely new. It just pulled together different parts of other laws.

However, the law was now very clear on two things. The burgesses might have argued about them:

1 The 1601 Poor Law said that there was a big difference between able-bodied poor people who really wanted work and **sturdy beggars** who were fit and well but refused to work.

2 All the better-off people in each parish now had to pay a tax, called the **Poor Rate**.

> This law is **much better**. Now we will only punish those who really need to be punished.

> I disagree! The new law is **not harsh enough** on the vagrants. It was better when we used to bore holes in their ears.

> The Poor Rate is a good idea. Many parishes already use this and **it works**.

> This is a **disaster!** Our grandfathers relied on the Christian duty and generosi[ty] of the rich citizens. Now th[e] whole city is responsible fo[r] the poor people! The poor will become lazier than ever.

The burgesses probably also argued about whether to spend money building more almshouses and hospitals for the sick or elderly poor people. And should they build a special place for the poor people who refused to work? Some cities, such as Norwich, had built special houses of correction. These were like prisons for poor people. The sturdy beggars would be kept there for about three weeks and would only receive food and drink if they did some work.

## What the burgesses did

In the end the burgesses of Bristol decided not to build any new almshouses or a house of correction. They decided that they would collect the Poor Rate and use it to help only the **deserving poor**, just as the Queen had ordered.

### Think

- What was the Poor Rate?
- What was a house of correction?
- Why might some people say it was better to bore a hole through a vagrant's ear than to whip him?

This would be expensive. They were therefore determined that **only the deserving poor born in Bristol** should be given help. They came up with a plan.

The burgesses appointed a special officer called a **Beadle of the Beggars**. It was his job to search for any 'vagrants, idle and disorderly people'. This beadle had so much to do that they soon had to appoint another beadle to help him! This second beadle was called the Beadle of the Rogues. He had to round up all the beggars who were thieves. The burgesses gave him whips and set up a cage to hold anyone he arrested.

*A print showing a beggar being whipped, made in 1577*

## Busy beadles

These beadles must have been very busy. Bristol was full of outsiders. Some had come just a few miles. Others came across the sea from Ireland. Anyone who allowed a stranger to live in their house was ordered to get rid of them or they would face a heavy fine. In 1605 the citizens of Bristol paid for 66 vagrants to be shipped back to Ireland.

One problem for the beadles was that it was hard to know which poor people were vagrants from elsewhere and which belonged to Bristol. So the burgesses ordered all poor people from Bristol who were receiving help to wear a special badge on their right shoulder. If they refused to wear the badge they would be punished as an ordinary vagrant. The badge had to be made of red or blue cloth. The badge for the parish of St Stephen's might have looked like this.

**STEP 2**

**Write a heading:** <u>Putting the 1601 Poor Law into practice</u>.
**Gather facts and ideas from the section called
'A new law arrives' (pages 27, 28 and 29) to make two lists:**

1   How some of the poor in Bristol were helped

2   How some of the poor in Bristol were punished

29

# An old problem remains

The next ninety years were not easy for Bristol, or for the rest of the country. Famine and plague kept returning. The number of poor people continued to rise. Some decided to leave the country for ever and go to America. But so many remained that the richer people had to pay more and more Poor Rate. This upset them. They said that some lazy poor now expected the parish to look after them.

In some parishes there were not enough rich people to be able to support the poor. In Elizabeth I's day, some parishes, like Temple or St Thomas', had been rich, but the woollen trade had gone bad. Some of the people who had been rich were now poor.

In 1680, a Bristol churchwarden called John Carey went to see the mayor. He said that the Poor Law was not working. Some parishes could not afford to help their poor. Others had money to spare. Also, churchwardens in each parish were finding it hard to run the system. Time and money were being spent moving vagrants from one parish to another inside the city.

Carey and the mayor agreed to make some changes. This is what they agreed to do:

1 All the parishes in Bristol would join together to deal with their poor.

2 Special officers would run the Poor Law instead of the churchwardens.

3 The mayor would decide how much Poor Rate each parish could afford to pay.

4 A new house of correction would be built – a **workhouse**. Anyone in Bristol who was unemployed but fit could be sent there and forced to work. This included children from families who could not afford to feed them properly.

In 1696 Bristol had its new workhouse. It had a special sign made. The sign showed a beehive surrounded by buzzing bees. Inside, there was a grim reminder that they were there to work. The new workhouse had a whipping post and a prison room complete with chains.

Hmm… We're going to have to make some changes.

What is wrong with the Poor Law : problem J.am

## Think

● Why do you think Carey wanted all the parishes in Bristol to join together to deal with the poor?

● Why do you think that a beehive was chosen as a sign for the workhouse?

Other cities were so impressed by Bristol's solutions that they copied them. Many towns and cities treated their poor people this way for the next hundred years. But the problem was not solved. The arguments continued.

**Write a heading:** The later seventeenth century. **Gather facts and ideas from page 30 to make two lists:**

1  How the poor of Bristol were helped

2  How the poor of Bristol were punished

# Thinking your enquiry through

1  Look carefully at the two lists which you have made in each Step.

- Take a green pen. Underline things which show that the way the poor were treated **stayed the same**.

- Take a red pen. Underline things which show **changes** in the way the poor were treated.

  Don't worry if you underline some facts in red **and** green. That is the whole point! We could say that things changed a lot or we could say that nothing very important changed at all. It all depends upon how you look at the problem.

2  Historians are always arguing about this kind of thing. Imagine that you are an historian. You have been asked to speak on the radio for just one minute. You have been invited to defend your recent book called, 'Beggars, Burgesses and Beadles in Bristol'. (Don't try to say that too quickly!)

Choose the statement below which you think **best** describes the treatment of poor people in sixteenth and seventeenth-century Bristol. There is no 'right' answer here. The statements just describe the developments differently. You must choose your statement and then **back it up** with two or three points from your lists.

## Statement 1

" The burgesses of Bristol carried on making the same mistakes. Sometimes they got tougher, sometimes they became fairer, but there was no big change. The burgesses carried on using the same mixture of help and punishment. They never tackled the real reasons why people became poor. "

## Statement 2

"The burgesses of Bristol were very creative. They could not solve the problem (because they did not understand why people became poor in the first place), but they did improve things. The system became fairer as they got used to telling the difference between different types of poor. It also became more efficient."

# A woman's life

## How can historians disagree when they are working with the same sources?

This is a puzzling picture. The man in the middle is Sir Richard Saltonstall. He is holding the hand of Richard, his son. The little girl is his daughter, Anne. Lying in bed is Lady Saltonstall. She was Sir Richard's first wife and the mother of Richard and Anne. **She is dead!** In the chair is Mary, Sir Richard's second wife. She is holding their new baby, Philip.

## Think

● Why is the picture puzzling?

● Why do you think Sir Richard had the picture painted?

Rich women, like Sir Richard Saltonstall's wives, usually got married in their early twenties. Sometimes they were not allowed to choose a husband for themselves. Instead, their parents decided who they should marry. Once they were married they had to stay married. Only the very rich could get divorced. We know that many women of all social classes spent much of their lives pregnant. People did not choose when they had babies in the sixteenth and seventeenth centuries!

But pregnancy and childbirth were dangerous in those days. Many women died in their thirties and forties. Marriages often ended because one of the partners died young.

Historians agree about these facts, but there is a lot which they cannot agree about. These two historians have very different ideas about what life was like for married women between 1500 and 1750.

## Interpretation 1

Married women in the sixteenth and seventeenth centuries had a very hard time. Wives had to obey their husbands. They were often treated badly. Wives were not free to do as they wanted. They spent all their time looking after their husbands and children.

## Interpretation 2

Married women had a lot more freedom than you think. Men and women were often equal partners in marriage. Husbands usually treated their wives well and women did not always obey their husbands. Married women did a lot of different jobs as well as looking after their families.

## Your enquiry

**These historians disagree about:**

1 the relationship between husbands and wives
2 the work that women did.

**Historians often disagree about the past. Sometimes they disagree because they start with different beliefs and views. Sometimes they disagree because they look at different sources. But in this enquiry you will see how two historians can disagree even when they are working with the same sources.**

# Domestic conduct books and advice manuals

In the sixteenth and seventeenth centuries some religious men wrote domestic conduct books like this one to tell husbands and wives how they should behave.

The books included pieces of advice like this:

Men should have power over their wives

Good wives should be patient, loving, sweet, kind and obedient

Men should look after their wives

Men should never hit their wives

Men should take advice from their wives

Men are stronger and wiser than women

Men should respect their wives

Wives should obey their husbands

> THE
> Proteſtant Monaſtery:
> OR,
> CHRISTIAN OECONOMICKS.
> CONTAINING
> Directions for the Religious Conduct
> of a FAMILY.
> By Sʳ Georye Wheeler.
> But as for me, and my houſe, we will ſerve the Lord: Joſh. XXIV. 15.
> Printed in the Year 1698.

## Think

- Which pieces of advice support Interpretation 1?

- Which pieces of advice support Interpretation 2?

- Which pieces of advice support both interpretations?

In the sixteenth and seventeenth centuries lots of people wrote books and cheap pamphlets to help people with the work they had to do. One of these books was Anthony Fitzherbert's 'Boke of Husbandry', written in 1523.

Here is some of his advice for a wife:

When you get up first sweep the house, set the table and put everything in your house in good order. Milk your cows, get your children up, dress them and make your husband's breakfast, dinner and supper. Send corn to the mill so that you can bake and brew whenever there is need. Make butter and cheese whenever you are able. Feed your pigs both morning and evening, and give your poultry their food in the morning.

At the beginning of March it is time for a wife to make her garden and to get as many good seeds and herbs as she can, especially those that be good for the pot and to eat. Make sure you weed your garden. March is also a good time to sow flax and hemp. From this you can make sheets, towels, shirts and smocks. A husband should have a sheep of his own, but the wife should have part of the wool to make her husband and herself some clothes.

It is a wife's job to winnow the grain, to wash and wring the clothes, to make hay, reap corn and to help her husband fill the muck cart, drive the plough and load hay and corn. It is her job to go to market to sell cheese, milk, eggs and to buy everything that is needed in the house. She must tell her husband what she has spent and the husband should do the same. Husband and wife will not prosper if they are not honest to each other.

## Think

- Which parts of Fitzherbert's book support Interpretation 1?

- Which parts of Fitzherbert's book support Interpretation 2?

- Does this source support one interpretation more than the other? If so, which one and why?

This is the front page of a seventeenth-century pamphlet. It was written by a woman and is a bit like a women's magazine today.

## Think

- Which pictures show the woman:
  making cheese?
  cooking?
  making medicine?
  preserving food?
  putting on make-up?

- How can you use the front page of this pamphlet to support both interpretations?

STEP 1

1 Copy this chart. Use the sources in the section called 'Domestic conduct books and advice manuals' to collect as much evidence as you can to support each interpretation.

|  | Evidence which supports Interpretation 1 | Evidence which supports Interpretation 2 |
|---|---|---|
| Domestic conduct books and advice manuals |  |  |

2 Does the evidence from domestic conduct books mostly support Interpretation 1 or Interpretation 2? Explain your answer.

# Pictures and descriptions

The trouble with domestic conduct books and advice manuals is that they only tell us how people **thought** husbands and wives should behave. We do not know whether people really took the advice and behaved in these ways. We need to look at other sources to find out. Pictures can help us with this. This picture is like a cartoon strip. It tells the story of something which happened to an ordinary couple in the seventeenth century.

*A Skimmington Ride, a plaster frieze from Montacute House, Somerset, early seventeenth century*

The wife beats her husband with a shoe – he has been drinking beer when looking after their baby.

Friends and neighbours put the husband on a pole and carry him around the village to make him look silly. Men are not supposed to let their wives hit them!

Other useful evidence about women's lives comes from the writings of foreign visitors. This is what a male Dutch visitor to England wrote in 1575:

## Think

- What does this picture tell you about the lives of poorer married women in the seventeenth century?

- How can you use the picture to support both interpretations?

Wives in England are entirely in the power of their husbands, yet they are not kept so strictly as in Spain. Nor are they shut up. They go to market. They are well dressed, fond of taking it easy and leave the care of the household to their servants. They spend time walking, riding, playing cards and visiting friends, talking to neighbours and making merry with them, and in childbirth and christenings. All this with the permission of their husbands. This is why England is called the paradise of married women.

1 Add the heading **Pictures and descriptions** to the chart you began in Step 1. Read the sources in the section called 'Pictures and descriptions' again and add more evidence to support Interpretation 1 and Interpretation 2.

2 Does the evidence from these pictures and descriptions mostly support Interpretation 1 or Interpretation 2? Explain your answer.

# Diaries

Some of the best sources for finding out about married women's lives are diaries. When you use diaries to find out about women's lives you need to remember two things:

1 Most diaries were written by men so you only get one side of the story.

2 Poorer people could not write, so diaries mostly tell us about the gentry and the middling sort of people.

One man who wrote a very detailed diary in the seventeenth century was Samuel Pepys. Here are some extracts from his diary. They tell us about his relationship with his wife:

## Think

- Which parts of the diary suggest that Pepys treated his wife badly?

- Which parts of Pepys' diary suggest that he and his wife were equal partners?

**2 May 1663**

I slept till almost 7 o'clock. Some angry words with my wife about her neglecting to keep the house clean, I calling her a 'beggar' and she calling me a 'prick-louse'. To my office. Home to dinner. Very merry and well pleased with my wife.

**19 December 1664**

I was very angry and began to find fault with my wife for not commanding the servants as she ought. She giving me a cross answer, I did strike her over her left eye such a blow as the poor wretch did cry out. But her spirit was such that she scratched and bit me.

**12 July 1667**

... And so to home, and there finding my wife in a bad mood for my not dining at home. I did give her a pull by the nose and left. She followed me in a devilish manner, so I got her into the garden out of hearing (to avoid shame) and managed to calm her. Then I walked with her in the garden, and so to supper, pretty good friends and so to bed.

Another man who kept a detailed diary in the seventeenth century was Adam Eyre. Adam was a yeoman farmer in Yorkshire. In 1647 he wrote in detail about his troubles with his wife Susan. Here is a summary of what went wrong:

## On 9 June 1647 ...

The couple had a big argument. Adam was not very good with money and wanted to sell some of his wife's land to pay off his debts. She refused to hand it over. Adam was very religious and wanted his wife to wear dull and decent clothes. She told him that her clothes were none of his business. Susan swore at her husband because he stood on her sore foot. Adam said he would not share a bed with her until she took more notice of him.

## On 30 July 1647 ...

Adam stayed at home all day because Susan would not let him go out and play bowls.

## On 6 August 1647 ...

Adam spent the evening wondering whether he should leave his wife. He got up in the middle of the night to pray and to ask God what he should do.

## During the autumn of 1647 ...

Adam stayed with Susan, but their arguments continued. In October he wrote in his diary that Susan had been 'very angry' and 'very angry all day'.

## On 1 January 1648 ...

It was a very stormy night. The chimney fell down. Adam thought that this was a sign of God being angry with him and he decided to make friends with his wife. He promised to be a good husband. Susan promised she would obey her husband but refused to hand over her land.

### Think

- Does Adam Eyre's diary entry for 1 January 1648 show that wives always obeyed their husbands?

## STEP 3

1 Add the heading <u>Diaries</u> to the chart you began in Step 1 and include examples from Pepys and Eyre which support Interpretation 1 and Interpretation 2.

2 Does the evidence from these diaries mostly support Interpretation 1 or Interpretation 2?

# What historians have found out ...

Historians often use other people's research to support their own interpretations. This is not cheating. It saves time and makes their arguments much stronger. Here are some research findings which you can use to support each interpretation:

About one in ten marriages ended with the husband running away from his wife and children.

The law said that as soon as a woman got married everything a woman owned became her husband's.

For most of the period 1500–1750, diaries tell us that married women spent their time at home, looking after children, cooking, fetching water, washing clothes and spinning.

When a husband wrote his will he usually left his wife everything he owned.

Diaries and letters show that many husbands and wives were very close and missed each other when they were apart.

Pictures sometimes show women carrying corn, shearing sheep, thatching, spreading manure and breaking stones for road repair.

**Court** records show that men were sometimes brought to court for beating their wives.

**STEP 4**

**Decide which of these findings you can use to support each interpretation. Add the heading _General findings_ to the chart you began in Step 1. Then put the findings in the correct column.**

## Thinking your enquiry through

**You are now going to write an essay to explain how historians disagree about the lives of married women. Use the information in your chart to back up your ideas. This writing frame will help you:**

Historians disagree about the lives of married women in the period 1500–1750.
Some historians think ...
Other historians think ...

Domestic conduct books and advice manuals can be used to support both interpretations. On one hand ...
On the other hand ...

The evidence from pictures and descriptions suggests that ...

Most of the evidence from diaries supports the view that ...

Historians will continue to disagree about the lives of married women because ...

# 'Revenge for revenge and blood for blood'

## 5

## Why was life so wild in the Anglo-Scottish borders?

During the summer of 1581 hundreds of men from the Elliott family were raiding the English borders. They moved about in bands of around a hundred men. They came from the valley of Liddesdale in Scotland. No one went near them. No one tried to challenge them. They stole 274 cattle and 12 horses. They destroyed nine houses, wounded three men and took one prisoner.

This valley is in the south of Scotland. It is wild and bleak. Around the border between Scotland and England much of the countryside looks like this. In the sixteenth century this valley was a good place for hiding stolen cattle.

Life was wild in the Anglo-Scottish borders. Anyone who lived there needed to know the local customs. Anyone who tried to control the people who lived there needed to know what he was letting himself in for.

## Your enquiry

The borders were controlled by wardens. There were wardens on both the Scottish side and on the English side. By the end of this enquiry you will know what a tough job it was to be a warden. You will be able to write to a new Scottish warden to warn him about the dangers he will face.

# Warlike behaviour in peacetime

The behaviour of the Elliotts in 1581 was not unusual. It was a typical summer's work. In the 1580s more than three thousand cattle were stolen, 66 buildings were destroyed, 14 men were murdered and 146 prisoners were kidnapped. On average, the Elliotts carried out one big raid every week. This was their way of life. It was called reiving. No cattle could be left unguarded. No one could travel in safety.

The Elliotts were just one family or **clan**. These families were known as the surnames or the 'riding surnames'. There were surname groups on both sides of the border.

These surnames were strong family groups. They had become very important in the fourteenth and fifteenth centuries. At that time, England and Scotland were often at war. Many raids took place across the border. Things often got out of hand. Families banded together for protection against enemy raiders.

But even when England and Scotland were not at war, the raiding carried on. This is a verse from a Scottish riding ballad. It shows how the **borderers** used the old hatred between Scotland and England as an excuse for raiding:

> Then Johnie Armstrong to Willie can say
> 'Billie a riding then will we.
> England and us has long been at feud.
> Perhaps we may hit off some booty.'

*From the ballad Dick o' the Cow, sixteenth-century riding ballad*

## Think

- What is Johnie Armstrong saying in the verse from the riding ballad?

- Why had the surname groups become so strong by the sixteenth century?

# The Anglo-Scottish marches and the surname groups

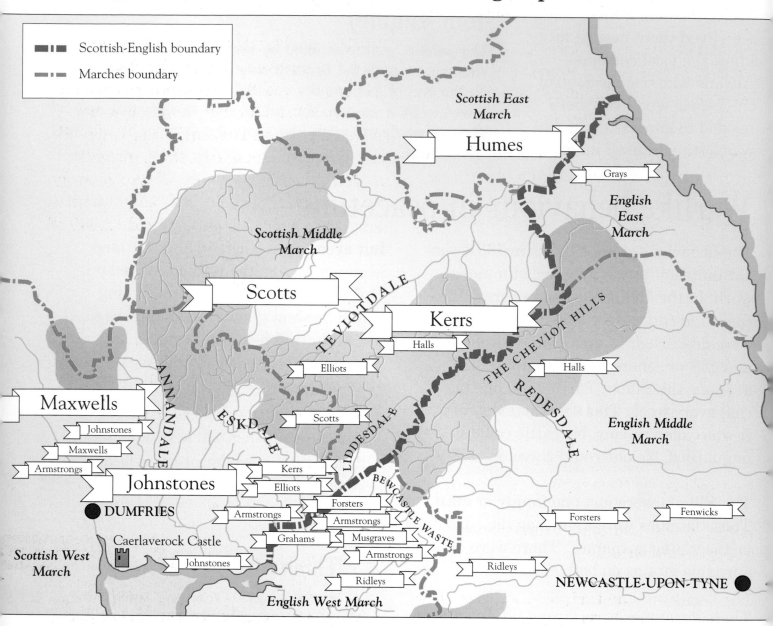

**Scottish-English boundary**

**Marches boundary**

Scottish East March

Humes

Grays

English East March

Scottish Middle March

Scotts

TEVIOTDALE

Kerrs

Halls

THE CHEVIOT HILLS

Elliots

Halls

REDESDALE

ANNANDALE

ESKDALE

Maxwells

Scotts

English Middle March

Johnstones

Maxwells

Armstrongs

Johnstones

LIDDESDALE

Kerrs

Elliots

Forsters

BEWCASTLE WASTE

DUMFRIES

Armstrongs

Armstrongs

Forsters

Fenwicks

Caerlaverock Castle

Grahams

Musgraves

Scottish West March

Johnstones

Armstrongs

Ridleys

Ridleys

NEWCASTLE-UPON-TYNE

English West March

This map shows the main surname groups. It also shows the different **marches**. This was the name given to the lands around the border. There were three marches on the Scottish side and three on the English side. The **wardens** of the marches were expected to control the local people and to prepare them for battle in time of war.

## Think

- Each of the marches had its own warden. How many wardens were there?

- Find three surname groups from the Scottish side and three surname groups from the English side.

- Look back at the verse from the riding ballad on page 41. How do you know that it was telling a story about the Scottish side of the border?

# Raiding and reiving – A way of life

For the borderers, violent raiding was normal. It was called reiving. Reiving included blackmail, kidnapping, cattle theft and killing people in family feuds.

Ordinary crime, however, was *not* accepted as normal. Any crime which had nothing to do with reiving was punished very severely. One of the English wardens, Robert Carey, was shocked by a new crime. He wrote in his memoirs:

> Two gentlemen thieves took purses from the travellers in the highways. This was a crime which had never been heard of in these parts before.

*Robert Carey's memoirs of the 1590s*

Robert Carey had these pickpockets hanged at Newcastle.

The borderers had their own standards of right and wrong. They saw things differently from other English and Scottish people. If you lived in the borders, you needed to know the difference.

Some historians used to think that Scotland was more violent than England. This is not very likely. Records kept at the time of Elizabeth I are very misleading.

People only **think** that the Scottish were more violent than the English because the English crime records are far more detailed. Other evidence gives a different picture. The English probably did just as much damage. In 1593, the valley of Liddesdale in Scotland suffered terribly. The men of Liddesdale did £3,230 worth of damage to England, but suffered £8,000 of damages in return.

Robert Carey wrote:

> The Scots have been used to rob and spoil, and think it their right, scorning all opposition. But the English are as bad or worse than the Scots.

*Robert Carey's memoirs of the 1590s*

## STEP 1

**Look carefully at pages 40 to 43. Find three reasons why life was wild in the Anglo-Scottish borders. Think about what the countryside was like, the history of the borders, the way society was organised and what the borderers believed. When you have found your three reasons, write them down.**

# Hot on their heels with a hot trod

Imagine you are a member of the Armstrongs. You live on the Scottish side. You have been raided by the Grahams from England. They have stolen all your cattle, burnt your buildings and terrified the Armstrong women. You have a number of options.

**Your options**

Will you:

1  set out at once with all the Armstrongs you can find, chase the Grahams, catch up with them and take back your stolen cattle by force

2  get the warden of the Scottish West March to carry out an official raid on the Grahams to punish them

3  take your time, wait until you have gathered a large band of Armstrongs, then take your revenge on the Grahams with a terrible raid on their homes – burning, terrorising, stealing and killing?

**Now make your choice.**

If you chose Option 1 you would have been on the right side of the law. All borderers were allowed to chase thieves and gain back their stolen property, as long as they did so soon afterwards. This was called a 'hot trod'. It was legal.

Option 2 was legal as well. In the early sixteenth century, the Scottish and English monarchs made a special agreement. If the local wardens were not able to sort out disagreements peacefully, they could get the permission of their king or queen to carry out an official raid over the border.

Option 3 was **not** allowed. Taking revenge was **not** like a hot trod. The borderers were not supposed to take revenge. Ever since the fourteenth century, there had been special treaties and laws stopping the borderers from taking revenge.

But this did not stop the borderers. They just took revenge anyway. By the end of the sixteenth century, some wardens saw revenge as the only way to keep some kind of order. In 1597 Robert Carey, the English warden, wrote:

> The best way to keep them quiet is to do one evil turn for another. I see no other way than revenge for revenge and blood for blood.

*Letter from Robert Carey to Lord Burghley, 1597*

The wardens just could not control the violence of the borderers. This is not surprising as they were usually part of it themselves.

Oh no! It's a hot trod!

44

# The impossible job of the wardens of the marches

The wardens of the marches had an impossible job. Even though England and Scotland were mostly at peace during the sixteenth century, kings and queens still expected the borderers to be ready to fight at all times (so who could blame them for being violent!).

In 1596, one of Elizabeth I's officials reminded the English wardens:

> It must not be forgotten how the marches are counties against another realm where men must be in military service, and defend when times shall need, and always, like marchers, be ready ...

But the trouble was that the Anglo-Scottish border was not terribly important to many local people. They did not really care who they were raiding. English surnames feuded with English surnames. Scottish surnames stole from Scottish surnames. Loyalty to family was much stronger than loyalty to country, king or queen.

Imagine you are the Scottish king. One of the wardens of your marches has died. You need a new one. You have a number of options.

**Your options**

Will you choose:

1 a powerful local man who will be highly respected by the local people (but will not take much notice of you)

2 a less powerful local man whom you will be able to control (but who may not be able to control the local people)

3 a complete outsider who will be able to keep out of all the borderers' quarrels and feuds?

**Now make your choice.**

If you chose Option 1 then you did what Scottish kings did, most of the time.
On the Scottish side the wardens usually came from the same families:

| | | |
|---|---|---|
| East March | – | the Humes |
| Middle March | – | the Kerrs |
| West March | – | the Maxwells |

This system still caused big problems. These families were mixed up in all the feuding. For example, the Maxwells and the Johnstones hated each other. When, in 1529, a Maxwell was made a warden, he was not allowed to deal with any problems which involved the Johnstones. The Maxwells could not be trusted to be fair.

Option 2 would be risky. The Scottish monarch might have been able to control a less powerful man, but the local surnames would take no notice of him.

45

Option 3 would be **a disaster**.
The story on the right shows you why:

*Caerlaverock Castle.*
*This was a Maxwell stronghold in the sixteenth century*

In 1516, a Frenchman, Anthony Darcy, was put in charge of the Scottish East March. This was where the Humes lived. The Humes hated him. They saw him as an outsider. They felt that he had no right to control them.

This unfortunate Frenchman worked very hard to govern the East March fairly and honestly. That made things even worse. This was not the kind of government the Scottish borderers were used to. One day, a large band of Humes rode out to capture Darcy. They cut off his head. They used Darcy's long hair to tie his head to one of their saddles. Then they rode all the way home with Darcy's head dangling for all to see.

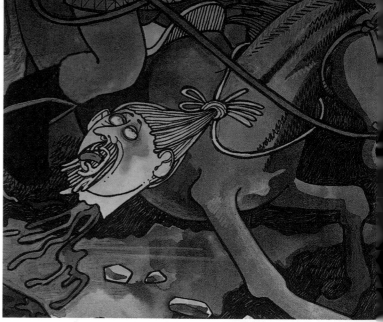

The English monarchs did things differently. They often chose outsiders as wardens. But these outsiders did not know the borderers' customs and ways. These wardens were often hated by the local English surnames. Some, like Robert Carey, were able to understand the borderers' way of life. But usually they stayed as outsiders. The local families did not co-operate.

But letters written by the English wardens show that it was something else which really annoyed them. English monarchs did not give their wardens the support which they needed. English monarchs did not really trust their wardens.

It also suited the English monarchs for the borders to be violent. Sometimes Henry VIII and Elizabeth I dealt very harshly with the law breakers on the English side. But sometimes they took advantage of the borderers' violence in their own quarrels with powerful nobles. Sometimes they even plotted with the Scottish surnames against their own people.

## STEP 3

Using pages 45 and 46, find at least three more reasons why life was wild in the Anglo-Scottish borders.

## Thinking your enquiry through

Imagine you are living in sixteenth-century Scotland. The Scottish king plans to appoint a new warden, **from outside the borders.** You must warn the new warden to be careful, and, if possible, not to take the job. Write a letter to him.

**You must warn the warden of these things:**

- Make sure that he knows the difference between reiving and 'ordinary' theft.
- Make sure that he knows the difference between a hot trod (which is legal) and taking revenge (which is illegal ... but everyone does it anyway).
- Make sure that he knows how violent the borderers are.
- Make sure he knows that he cannot rely on the Scottish people to be on his side.

**Explain all these things carefully. Make your warning clear. Remember, you want to put him off! Tell him a few lively stories just in case he still has not got the message.**

# Breaking the border

All of this enquiry was about the sixteenth century. The seventeenth century saw a very different story. In 1603, Elizabeth I of England died without any children. James VI of Scotland became James I of England as well. Now that he ruled both kingdoms he did not expect them to be at war with each other. He was determined to end the wild behaviour of the borderers.

James VI and I ended the old system of wardens and marches. As for the borderers, he was ruthless. He wanted to sweep away their whole way of life. He did not waste any time. In 1603, 32 Elliotts, Armstrongs and Johnstones were hanged. Fifteen were banished and 140 were outlawed. This was only the beginning. Many borderers were hanged. Whole families were **exiled** and sent to Ireland. Harsh new laws were made, like this one:

> If any Englishman steal in Scotland, or any Scotsman steal in England any goods or chattels amounting to 12 pence, he shall be punished by death.

*Border Commissioners, 1605*

## The breaking of the borders had begun.

| James IV | James V | Mary, Queen of Scots | James VI |
|---|---|---|---|
| 1488–1513 | 1513–1542 | 1542–1567 | 1567–1625 |

Mary, Queen of Scots executed by her cousin Queen Elizabeth in 1587

# Chopping and changing

## 6

## What happened when Henry VIII took control of the Church?

When Henry VIII became king in 1509, one nobleman said he could feel heaven rejoicing. People often feel full of hope when there is a chance for a new start. Henry VIII's father was Henry VII. He had been a strong king who had settled the country down after the Wars of the Roses, but he seemed rather dull. No one could say that about his son, Henry VIII. This famous painting from the sixteenth century reminds us how powerful Henry VIII was by the middle of his reign.

Henry VIII could use his great power to change the lives of his people. He certainly changed the lives of all the people whose heads rolled off the chopping block during his reign. Many of them had once been very close to Henry. They had been wives, advisers or friends.

## How things change!

*Henry VIII*

**1535 – The Bishop of Rochester, leading member of the Church**
'Off with his head!'

**1535 – Thomas More, a close friend and adviser**
'Off with his head!'

**1536 – Anne Boleyn, his second wife**
'Off with her head!'

**1540 – Thomas Cromwell, his chief adviser**
'Off with his head!'

**1542 – Catherine Howard, his fifth wife**
'Off with her head!'

When Henry took the throne in 1509 many people thought he was a perfect king. He agreed with them. He insisted that they must call him 'Your Majesty', a title which English kings had never used before. The **Pope** soon gave him a new title too. He called Henry the 'Defender of the Faith' because Henry was such a good Roman Catholic. But – as the picture reminds us – things change.

## Your enquiry

In this enquiry you will learn how Henry VIII used his power to make the greatest of all his changes – he ended the power of the Roman Catholic Church in England. We call this the 'Break with Rome'. It changed the whole history of Britain. You face a difficult challenge. You must explain these complicated events so clearly that a primary school pupil can understand them.

# The causes – Why Henry VIII made the Break with Rome

Some say that Henry only made the Break with Rome because the Pope would not let him have a divorce. In 1509, Henry married a Spanish princess called Catherine of Aragon. She had once been the wife of his brother, Arthur, who was now dead. The Bible seemed to say that a man should never marry his brother's widow, but the Pope gave permission for the marriage to go ahead.

By 1526 the marriage had gone badly wrong. In 1527, Henry asked the Pope to let him divorce Catherine but the Pope refused, no matter how often Henry asked.

The problem was that Henry needed a son to take the throne after he died. By 1526 Catherine had suffered several miscarriages and five other children had been still-born or had died as infants. She had only one healthy child, a daughter called Mary. Since 1518 Catherine had not even been pregnant. Henry wondered if God was punishing him for marrying Catherine.

*The coronation of Henry VIII and Catherine of Aragon in 1509*

Oh dear … perhaps God is angry with me.

Henry was especially keen to divorce Catherine because he had fallen madly in love with Anne Boleyn, a young lady at his court. Henry desperately wanted her hand in marriage (despite the fact that it had six fingers!).

Henry was sure that Anne would be able to give him a son but the Pope still refused to let him divorce Catherine. Between 1527 and 1533 Henry grew more and more impatient. He simply had to find a way to divorce Catherine and to marry Anne.

## Think

- When did Henry marry Catherine?
- Why did Henry ask for a divorce in 1527?

At that time a growing number of English people were **Protestants**. Anne came from a Protestant family. Protestants protested against the **Roman Catholic** Church which seemed to have too much power over England. Not only did the Pope interfere with the king's marriage plans, but he also took English Church taxes. Some rulers in Germany had managed to end the Pope's power over their people. Henry liked the sound of this. Why should the Pope, a foreign Church leader, have so much control over England?

Protestants also complained that the Roman Catholic Church was rich and **corrupt**. Reports proved that many priests and monks were greedy and sinful (although some did live very simple, holy lives). The **monasteries** were very wealthy. They owned huge areas of land in England and collected rents from these lands. They also had beautiful treasures made of gold and silver. Henry badly needed money to pay for the wars he had been fighting in France.

Why should such a wicked Church be so rich when **I** need the money so badly?

Henry knew he would be popular with the Protestants if he changed church services in England. Protestants believed that the Roman Catholic Church had grown **superstitious**. They said services should be in English and that priests should use the Bible to explain true faith to the people. Henry did not really agree with all these new teachings – but he would put up with them if it meant he could control the Church and get his divorce.

## Think

- Why did Protestants want to break away from the Roman Catholic Church?

- How fair do you think it would be to call Henry VIII a Protestant?

*Thomas Cromwell*

*Thomas Cranmer*

By 1533 two of Henry's most important advisers were encouraging him to start a new Church of England. Thomas Cromwell more or less ran the government for Henry. Thomas Cranmer was the new Archbishop of Canterbury. Both men were Protestants.

They told the king what he wanted to hear: that the Pope should have no power over England and that Henry should run both the government and the Church. The king was delighted, especially as Anne Boleyn was now pregnant and he had to marry her soon.

## STEP 1

**By the end of 1533 Henry had made the decision to break away from the Roman Catholic Church. You have read about several reasons why he did this. Copy this chart:**

| | The causes – Why Henry VIII made the Break with Rome |
|---|---|
| Love | |
| Money | |
| Faith | |
| Power | |

Now go back through this section (pages 49, 50 and 51). Note down on the chart any reasons to do with Love which made Henry break away from the Roman Catholic Church. Then do the same for Money, Faith and Power.

# The change –
# How Henry VIII made the Break with Rome

Henry used Parliament to help him make the Break with Rome. If Parliament passed Henry's changes then he could claim that everyone agreed with them. In this way, Henry helped to make Parliament feel more powerful than ever – without meaning to.

Between 1529 and 1536 Parliament passed many laws. Some had nothing to do with the Break with Rome. For example, Parliament united Wales and England by making them share the same system of law and local government.

But Parliament's real task was to cut the links between Rome and England. The most important new law that it passed was the Act of Supremacy (1534). This said that Henry was the head of the new Church of England. All church services were now in English and a copy of the Bible in English was placed in each church.

Most people accepted these new rules but some did not. If someone obeyed the Pope rather than the king it was an act of treason and the punishment was death. Bishop John Fisher and Henry's close friend and adviser, Thomas More, were among the first of many to be executed.

Henry closed down the monasteries. He took all their property and sold it to landowners and merchants. Gold and silver ornaments were melted down and beautiful old books were burnt. The buildings were turned into private houses or left to crumble.

This picture was made in 1534. The artist has tried to sum up the changes that Henry VIII was making.

## Think

- Find Pope Clement, two of Henry's Protestant advisers, a copy of the Bible, and some worried monks

- Bishop Fisher was on the Pope's side. How has the artist shown this?

**Make your own copy of this diagram.**
**In each of the boxes do a simple drawing to illustrate what Henry did.**

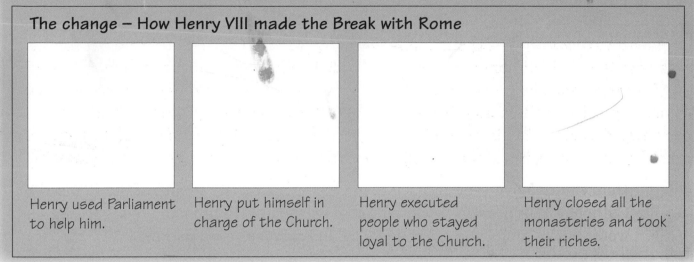

The change – How Henry VIII made the Break with Rome

| Henry used Parliament to help him. | Henry put himself in charge of the Church. | Henry executed people who stayed loyal to the Church. | Henry closed all the monasteries and took their riches. |

# The consequences – What happened after Henry VIII made the Break with Rome

As some of Henry's wives, friends and advisers found out, things don't always turn out as people expect. Henry soon discovered this too.

Henry divorced Catherine of Aragon and married Anne Boleyn in 1533. Three months later Anne had Henry's child. Henry was sure it would be a son.

But he was **wrong!** It was a girl, Elizabeth. Almost immediately, Henry began to hate Anne as much as he had once loved her. Soon, he heard stories that she was having affairs with other men at court. That was enough. He had her executed.

Henry's third wife, Jane Seymour, finally gave him the son he so desperately wanted – even though she died in childbirth. That son was Henry's last child. He became Edward VI when Henry died in 1547.

## Think

- Henry had three more wives after Jane Seymour died. None of them had any children. How much do you think this mattered to Henry?

With a son to follow him, Henry believed that his new Church of England was safe. Edward was brought up as a Protestant so Henry must have been sure that the Pope would never again have power over England.

If he thought this, he was **wrong again!** Edward died as a teenager and Mary, Edward's half-sister, took over as queen. Mary was a Catholic. She ended the Church of England and made England Catholic once again! When Mary died in 1558 Henry's third child, Elizabeth, became queen. She made the country Protestant again, but for hundreds of years afterwards the country was divided by religion. What a mess.

Henry must have been pleased to get his hands on the wealth of the Roman Catholic Church when he closed the monasteries. He probably thought this would make kings and queens of England rich for years to come.

But he was **wrong again!** He sold most of the land and property that belonged to the monasteries and then wasted the money on wars in the years that followed. Poor old Henry. If only he had known.

Henry wanted to use the Break with Rome to make himself the undisputed king of his country. He was sure that kings would be more powerful than ever once their old rival, the Pope, no longer had any power over them.

He was **wrong again!** Roman Catholics kept trying to get back into power. Almost every single English monarch between 1534 and 1750 had to deal with some sort of Catholic plot or war. Instead of uniting the kingdom, religion was dividing it.

Of course, Henry VIII had not really planned to cause any of these problems. It just goes to show, as you saw at the start of the enquiry, that things in history did not always turn out as people expected.

*Lacock Abbey in Wiltshire*
*An example of an abbey that was turned into a rich man's home*

Copy this chart and fill it in. At first Henry seemed to get what he wanted in Love, Money, Faith and Power, but this did not last. Use facts from this section (pages 53 and 54) to show what went wrong for Henry.

The consequences – What happened after Henry VIII made the Break with Rome

| What Henry wanted | What Henry did | What went wrong for Henry |
|---|---|---|
| Love | He married Anne Boleyn ... | but ... |
| Money | He closed all the monasteries and took their riches ... | but ... |
| Faith | He ... | but his new Church was more Protestant than he really wanted. |
| Power | He gave English monarchs power over a Protestant country ... | but ... |

# Thinking your enquiry through

**Write a very simple booklet for primary school children about the Break with Rome. It must have three main sections.**

1 The first section must explain why Henry made the Break with Rome. Remember to mention Love, Money, Faith and Power. The chart you made in Step 1 will help you.

2 The second section must describe how he made the Break with Rome. You could write about each of the pictures you did in Step 2.

3 The third section must say what happened as a consequence (result) of the Break with Rome. The chart you made in Step 3 will help you.

# Queen and country

## How did Elizabeth control her people?

In 1588, the King of Spain sent his famous **Spanish Armada** of fighting ships to conquer England. It failed completely. The English queen, Elizabeth I, had this painting made to celebrate England's success.

*The Armada Portrait*

### Think

- Which two parts of the painting show the Spanish Armada arriving and being destroyed?

- How does the artist make Elizabeth look calm?

- How does the artist make her look powerful?

56

## Your enquiry

In this enquiry you will follow the story of Elizabeth's quarrels with Spain. You will have to make some important decisions as if you are advising the Queen. By the end of the enquiry you should be an expert on the difficult problems that almost all kings and queens faced.

# Keeping the faith

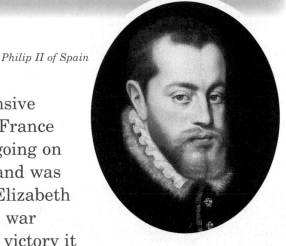

*Philip II of Spain*

Elizabeth's quarrels with Spain started soon after she became queen in 1558. King Philip II of Spain asked to marry her. This caused a problem.

Mary I had just died. She had upset many of her people. She had been a Roman Catholic and had undone all Henry VIII's changes to the Church – this angered English Protestants. She had started a war with France – England was losing badly. And she had made one other unpopular decision – she had married a rich, powerful, foreign king: Philip II of Spain. Now this same man wanted to marry Elizabeth.

The expensive war with France was still going on and England was broke. If Elizabeth ended the war without a victory it would be a bad start to her reign. Philip promised to use Spain's armies to help her against the French ... **if** she married him. The English expected her to marry someone and to have children. But Elizabeth was a Protestant and Philip was a Catholic. He was unpopular in England. Besides, he might take away some of her power. She faced a difficult decision.

## STEP 1

Elizabeth had a small team of hand-picked advisers called the Privy Council. She encouraged them to speak their mind but this could sometimes be dangerous. She once threw a shoe at one adviser and punched another on the ear!

Like many monarchs, Elizabeth faced serious problems over marriage and religion. Imagine you are one of Elizabeth's Privy Councillors.

1 List some reasons why Elizabeth should marry Philip.

2 List some reasons why she should not marry him.

3 Write down what you would advise her to do.

Did you advise Elizabeth to marry Philip or not? Whichever you chose, she would have been furious. You had no right to advise her about marriage! That was for her alone to decide. (Watch out for flying slippers.)

Elizabeth turned down Philip II's proposal of marriage, insulting the most powerful man in the world. She ended the war with France and made England Protestant again.

# Keeping the peace

In 1559, Elizabeth passed laws which put her in charge of the Church of England. She ordered everyone to attend Church of England services. These were in English but they kept some Catholic traditions. Elizabeth was trying to find a 'middle way' to keep both Catholics and Protestants happy. Her chief adviser, William Cecil, once explained that:

> A country cannot be safe where there are two religions. Those who differ in their service of God, can never agree in the service of their country.

*From a speech by William Cecil, December 1580*

If Catholics did not go to church Elizabeth simply fined them. She ordered the **Justice of the Peace (JP)** for each village to keep a record of those who missed church services. The JP kept law and order in the parishes in his area. He was not voted into power by the people. He was chosen by the Privy Council, who usually gave the job to

the richest landowner in the area. JPs were not paid, even though they were very busy.

There was no police force in Tudor times but JPs and others acted as spies for the Privy Council. The Privy Council needed these spies to catch traitors.

In 1580 the Pope ordered young English Catholic priests, called Jesuits, to make England Catholic again. Many Jesuits were captured, tortured and put to death as traitors. The law said that a traitor must be executed in this way:

> Let the traitor be hanged, taken down alive, his bowels taken out and burned before his face, and quartered.

Fierce punishments were often used in those days. Poisoners were boiled to death!

*A print from the sixteenth century showing the execution of a Jesuit*

## Think

- What is happening in the picture?
- Why were Jesuit priests seen as traitors?
- Why were Justices of the Peace important?

Some Catholics plotted to kill Elizabeth. They wanted Mary, Queen of Scots to rule England. She was next in line to the throne – and she was a Catholic.

In 1568 Mary had been forced to leave Scotland by Protestant nobles and she fled to England. Elizabeth kept her prisoner for nineteen years.

Parliament kept telling Elizabeth to execute Mary, but Elizabeth hesitated. Mary said she knew nothing about the plots.

Part of the problem was that she was Scottish and could not be tried by an English court. Besides, Mary was a queen, chosen by God. If Elizabeth did execute her, what might powerful Catholic enemies like Spain do? On the other hand, while Mary was alive the plots would continue. In 1586, Elizabeth's spies showed her proof that Mary had been plotting to kill her – but she knew that they had tricked Mary into joining the plot.

**STEP 2**

**Like many monarchs at that time, Elizabeth faced a plot against her. Imagine you are one of Elizabeth's Privy Councillors.**

1 List some reasons why Elizabeth should execute Mary.

2 List some reasons why she should not execute her.

3 Write down what you would advise Elizabeth to do.

# Defending the nation

In 1587, Elizabeth finally signed Mary's death warrant. One of her advisers sent it to the castle where Mary was a prisoner. She was executed the next morning. When Elizabeth heard this she went into a rage. She blamed the Privy Council for Mary's death, saying that she had never intended to send the death warrant.

Philip II of Spain thought Elizabeth must be punished. He had not forgiven her for refusing to marry him. He was also angry because English sailors such as Francis Drake had been robbing Spanish treasure ships. Philip decided that the time had come to teach Elizabeth a lesson. He drew up his plan to attack England with a massive sailing fleet – the Armada. Elizabeth was soon planning how to defend England.

## The Spanish plans of attack

1 Build a fleet of 130 warships

2 Gather an army of 35,000 men in the Netherlands, just across the English Channel

3 Sail the Armada from Spain to the Netherlands and carry the soldiers from the Netherlands to England

4 Depend mainly on the famous power of Spain's land forces

5 Pray for God's help

## The English defence plans

1 Order traders and fishermen to bring over 150 ships to join Elizabeth's navy of 28 warships at Plymouth

2 Order noblemen, called **Lords Lieutenant**, to train small bands of men to defend the coast in each county

3 Gather an army of about 5,000 men to defend London

4 Depend mainly on the famous skills of England's sailors

5 Pray for God's help

## Think

● Compare the two plans. Do you think that Elizabeth would have been confident that the English would beat the Spanish?

This map shows what happened to the Spanish Armada when it finally attacked in 1588. By November the English were celebrating victory. Here is how one writer at the time described the celebrations in London:

> The Queen and a gallant band of nobles went in triumph through the streets of London to St Paul's Church and gave thanks to God alone.

*From Camden's 'History of Princess Elizabeth'*

But even now the English could not be sure when the Spanish would return. Elizabeth had to decide whether she should let the English sailors go to their homes. As long as they were on the ships she had to pay their wages.

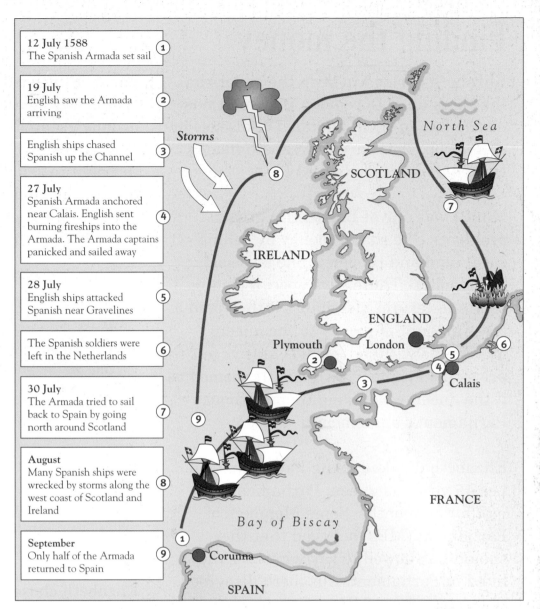

**1** 12 July 1588
The Spanish Armada set sail

**2** 19 July
English saw the Armada arriving

**3** English ships chased Spanish up the Channel

**4** 27 July
Spanish Armada anchored near Calais. English sent burning fireships into the Armada. The Armada captains panicked and sailed away

**5** 28 July
English ships attacked Spanish near Gravelines

**6** The Spanish soldiers were left in the Netherlands

**7** 30 July
The Armada tried to sail back to Spain by going north around Scotland

**8** August
Many Spanish ships were wrecked by storms along the west coast of Scotland and Ireland

**9** September
Only half of the Armada returned to Spain

### The route of the Spanish Armada

**STEP 3**

**Many monarchs had to make difficult decisions in times of war. Imagine you are one of Elizabeth's Privy Councillors. Use the map to help you.**

1 List some reasons why Elizabeth should let her sailors go home in September 1558.

2 List some reasons why she should not let them go home in September 1558.

3 Write down what you would advise her to do.

# Finding the money

Elizabeth decided to keep the sailors on the ships until December. By Christmas nearly half of them had died of disease or starvation. This saved Elizabeth money. Dead sailors needed no pay.

Money was one of Elizabeth's greatest problems. She raised money by selling royal land and property. She also sold 'monopolies'. These gave special trading rights to certain merchants if they paid a large amount of money to the queen. Merchants with monopolies always put the prices up. People were angry. It seemed as if the queen was taxing them without Parliament's agreement.

Elizabeth disliked using Parliament. In her 45 years as queen, Parliament only met for 36 months. Some Members of Parliament (MPs) believed that they should be allowed to say whatever they liked in Parliament. Elizabeth disagreed. She sent several MPs to prison when they criticised her plans.

*A print of Elizabeth I in Parliament, 1573–1578*

Elizabeth needed Parliament to raise taxes for the war against Spain. Parliament usually granted the taxes but it hated monopolies. Everyone knew the queen had the right to sell monopolies and that she needed the money, but it did not seem fair. People were angry at high prices and high taxes. Elizabeth was risking her popularity.

## STEP 4

**Most monarchs quarrelled with Parliament over taxes. Imagine you are one of Elizabeth's Privy Councillors.**

1 List some reasons why Elizabeth should keep using monopolies.

2 List some reasons why she should give them up.

3 Write down what you would advise Elizabeth to do.

Elizabeth chose to give up many of her monopolies. She seemed to be giving in to the MPs. However, she kept their respect by making a special speech to Parliament. One of the MPs wrote:

> Her well-chosen words, so learnedly composed, did delight her hearers with admiration.

Elizabeth had great power but she never forgot that she needed the respect and support of her people. It was a lesson which the next two kings – James I and Charles I – never learnt.

# Her Majesty

Throughout her reign Elizabeth used **propaganda** (one-sided messages) to show her people how good and powerful she was. Even church services included propaganda. People thanked God and prayed for her every Sunday.

Elizabeth also used paintings, like the *Armada Portrait*, to impress her subjects. The paintings were hung in the houses of important families all over the country.

Elizabeth also liked to show people what a fine queen she was by going on special journeys called 'Progresses'. She stayed with wealthy families. She visited one nobleman for three days and brought with her 300 carts and 2,400 horses. While her group was there it ate 196 kg of butter and 2,522 eggs!

Another nobleman, the Earl of Hertford, tried hard to impress the queen when she visited him in 1591. He created this huge man-made lake. The lake was used for plays, fireworks and other entertainments.

## Think

- How is the Queen being entertained?
- How would a nobleman feel if the Queen chose to stay with him?

## Thinking your enquiry through

Elizabeth had no children so the new king, James I, came from Scotland. He was not used to English ways. Imagine you are still a Privy Councillor. Prepare a speech to the new king.

**The speech should have two parts. Part one could start like this:**

Your Majesty, I beg to tell you that this is not an easy land to rule. Our dear Queen Elizabeth faced many difficulties. For example ...

(Give examples about marriage, religion, plots, wars, Parliament and money.)

**Part two could start like this:**

However, I am pleased that there are many things which may help Your Majesty to rule this land. For example Queen Elizabeth used ...

(Give examples about the Privy Council, Justices of the Peace, the Lords Lieutenant, the navy, Parliament, propaganda and God's support.)

# 'A thing most horrible'

## How did Charles I lose control?

In 1642, a wealthy Buckinghamshire landowner called Edmund Verney sent this letter to his brother Ralph. The letter was written just as Britain was about to enter nine years of **civil war**.

> Brother, what I feared is true – you are against the king. It breaks my heart to think that my father and I, who love you so dearly, should be your enemy because of our duty to the king. I am so troubled that I can write no more.

All wars bring pain and suffering but civil wars seem to hurt more than others. They are fought by people from the same country. As Edmund Verney discovered, they split families: fathers fight sons; brothers kill brothers; friends kill friends. Other comments from the time of the English Civil War show how people hated to fight their own countrymen. One general simply described civil war as 'a thing most horrible'.

## Your enquiry

You face a difficult challenge. You have to explain why people ended up fighting a war which they did not want. Most events in history – especially huge and powerful struggles like this civil war – have very complicated causes. You will have to make sense of several different causes which had built up over many years. Will you be able to sort them out?

Below is a short play. There are just two people in the play. They are two brothers like Edmund and Ralph. They are called Walter and Henry.

> I support King Charles I. Parliament has no right to fight against him.

This is Walter. He is a Royalist – he supports Charles I.

> I support Parliament. The king has no right to rule without Parliament's advice.

This is Henry. He supports Parliament.

## As you read the play, look for clues about the causes of the English Civil War.

The action takes place in August 1642, just as the English Civil War is about to start. Walter and Henry are arguing. Henry has blamed Charles I for causing the war. As the play begins, Walter is defending Charles.

# Walter and Henry – Part I

WALTER

You cannot blame King Charles for this war. He has made mistakes in the past but now he is just gathering his army at Nottingham so he can stand up for his rights.

HENRY

**His rights!** What about the rights of his people? Parliament is gathering its armies to protect the people against the king.

WALTER

The king means no harm to his people. But that awful Member of Parliament John Pym has led Parliament astray. How dare he raise an army to attack his own king? It is treason.

HENRY

But Pym had no choice! The king was the first to attack. Remember the 4th of January of this year, 1642? Charles disgraced himself when he took soldiers and forced his way into the House of Commons.

**WALTER**

Charles was only trying to arrest Pym and four other Members of Parliament. Why shouldn't he?

**HENRY**

No king has ever dared to do such a thing. I thank God that Pym and the others escaped. Our speaker knelt before the King and tried to show respect. But most of us just stared in amazement. With that attack, King Charles declared war on his people.

# Think

- Which side does Walter support?
- Which side does Henry support?
- How did Charles I upset Parliament in January 1642?

**HENRY**

The trouble is that King Charles wants all power for himself. He wants to keep the people like slaves. Parliament is fighting for their freedom.

**WALTER**

Nonsense! Our king has no wish to make us slaves – but nor does he want to be the slave of Parliament. He is a king, not a puppet. That is why he had to try to arrest those five MPs. They had gone too far.

**HENRY**

Whatever do you mean?

**WALTER**

They humiliated the king in October 1641 when they said he would not be allowed to lead an army. He needed that army to crush the Catholic rebels who are out of control in Ireland.

**HENRY**

Is that really why he wanted the army? Some of us believe he was going to use it against Parliament. Would his own Catholic wife have let him make war on Catholics in Ireland. No. She would have turned the king and his army against us. This king rules as he pleases.

**WALTER**

How could he? Parliament was taking away all his power. The MPs had told the king he could not collect any taxes without asking their permission. And in May 1641 they executed his chief minister, Strafford, without even finishing his trial. It seems to me that it is Parliament that wants to rule as it pleases.

**HENRY**

Parliament simply wants the king to rule with the advice and agreement of his people. That is why it had to stop him collecting taxes without asking Parliament's permission. When he finally called a Parliament in 1640, it was the first time it had been allowed to meet for 11 years! Before then that **tyrant** the Earl of Strafford had been **cheating** and **squeezing tax** from the people. I weep no tears for his death. He led the king astray. Pym was voted fairly into Parliament by men of wealth and property. Strafford was just a favourite of the king. We thought Charles would rule more sensibly without him – it seems we were wrong.

These three pictures show some events that Walter and Henry mentioned in the first part of the play. Study them carefully. Use the play to work out which event each picture shows and when each event happened.

*A print made in 1642*

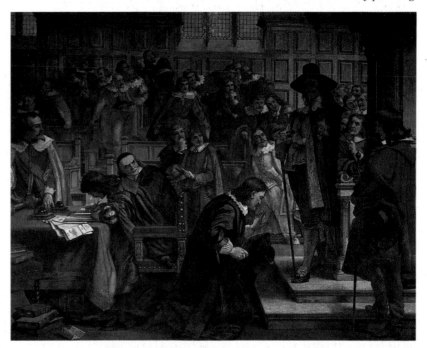

*A nineteenth-century painting*

*A seventeenth-century print showing an event in 1641*

# Walter and Henry – Part II

WALTER

## There you go again – blaming the king!

Of course he ruled without Parliament. He had no choice. Whenever he called a Parliament most of the MPs just tried to cut his power. He wouldn't have called a Parliament at all if there had not been a real emergency. If his ungrateful Scottish subjects had not attacked England in 1639, he would not have needed to pay for an army to get rid of them. Only Parliament could raise extra taxes – and it let him down. Shame on you for taking its side.

HENRY

I feel no shame. The king was ruining England and Scotland. Just think why those Scots rioted in their churches and attacked England in the first place. They were furious because the king and that fool Archbishop Laud forced them to use a Prayer Book.

WALTER

Just as we do here in England.

HENRY

Yes, but everyone knows the Scots would rather **die** than accept the Prayer Book. It reminded them of the old Roman Catholic ways. Maybe they were right. Look how the king and his archbishop changed our church services and buildings here in England. They are becoming more and more like those Catholic churches which the king's Catholic wife loves so much.

## Think

- What did the Scots do that forced Charles to call a Parliament?
- How had Charles upset the Scots?

WALTER

Careful my brother. You must not speak ill of our queen.

HENRY

But she has been part of the problem since she married Charles in 1625. We have never trusted her since she came from France with all her Catholic ways. And Archbishop Laud is little better. Many MPs are Puritans and proud of it. They know how Laud punishes any Puritans who dare to criticise him. They saw their Puritan friends after Laud had their ears sliced from their heads in 1637 – but they **will not** give in. Parliament will not stand by and let the king, the queen and Archbishop Laud turn our country Catholic again.

WALTER

King Charles is a true Protestant and so is Archbishop Laud. They love the Church of England. They just want church buildings to show the beauty of God. They do not trust Puritans who want bare buildings and who like to invent their own prayers and church rules. Puritans even want to choose their own Church leaders. They want to do away with bishops.

HENRY

But why is that so terrible?

WALTER

It must not happen. Charles' father, King James, always said that if Puritans did away with bishops they would soon do away with kings. That is why they must be punished. God has placed King Charles in charge of the Church and the country to keep good order and justice.

## Think

- How did Puritans think Church leaders should be chosen?

- What made King James think that Puritans might try to do away with kings?

HENRY

**Justice!** Is **that** what we had in our eleven years without a Parliament? It was a sad day in 1629 when King Charles decided to rule without Parliament. Yes, life went on quietly enough – but we saw what the king was doing. We watched as he found crafty ways of raising money to spend on his own family, his grand buildings and his priceless paintings.

WALTER

He had to find more money. He collects no more tax than kings did over a hundred years ago, but everything costs so much more now.

HENRY

You may be right, but look how he did it! He fined people who had done no wrong. He interfered with trade. And what about Ship Money? That tax was only supposed to come from ports when England was in danger of attack from the sea. In 1635 King Charles collected it from everywhere, when the country was perfectly safe! Was that justice?

These three pictures are connected with events mentioned by Walter and Henry in the second part of the play. Study them carefully. Work out what each picture shows and when each event happened.

*A portrait painted in the seventeenth century*

*A print made in the 1630s*

*A Proclamation (order) from Charles I in the 1630s*

# Walter and Henry – Part III

WALTER

Charles was just using his age-old rights as king when he collected the Ship Money. Why did that fool John Hampden make such a fuss about it by refusing to pay and going to court? It just stirred people up against the king – and it landed Hampden in prison. He is another of those Puritan MPs. They think they have the right to say whatever they like in Parliament.

HENRY

And so they do! MPs have been doing more and more to advise kings and queens ever since the days of Henry VIII. It is their **duty to serve their nation** by speaking the truth.

WALTER

**It is their duty to serve their king!** Those Puritans are just troublemakers. King James warned Charles that he would have trouble with Parliament. They had nothing like it in Scotland where King James was ruling before he came here to take our English throne.

HENRY

Exactly! These Stuart kings have forgotten that England is different from Scotland and other nations. We say that the king must rule with the agreement of Parliament. That is how men of property can have their say. They pay the taxes so they must have some control over how the money is spent. For a hundred years or more, families such as ours have been working hard to increase our wealth. It is only right that we also increase our power. King James tried to rule without Parliament. That is why our MPs were so firm with Charles at the very start of his reign.

## Think

- Why did English men of property think they should have some power in Parliament?

WALTER

There you go again! It is not for us to tell our king what he must do. It is our duty to serve him. I know he has made mistakes. But if we fail in our duty to him, we fail in our duty to God. Charles is always reminding us how his father once told him that 'God has made you a little god, to sit on the throne and to rule over other men'. I beg you brother – do your duty to the little god.

HENRY

**A little god! Never.**
Even our great Queen Elizabeth never claimed to be a goddess. She argued with Parliament, but she knew that Parliament could not be ignored. This king should learn from her wisdom. He is no little god. He is a great fool. And I fear, dear brother, that he has led you and me and all his people to the edge of a bloody civil war. It is a thing most horrible. May God forgive him.

WALTER

And may God forgive us, dear brother. May God forgive us.

This seventeeth-century picture shows King James I talking to his son Charles in 1621. Use Part III of the play to list some ideas about what King James might have been saying to Charles. What kinds of warnings and advice did he give to his son?

# The end of the English Civil War

The war started in August 1642. By the end of 1645 Parliament was clearly winning. In 1647 the King was captured. There was another short burst of fighting in 1648. Then, in 1649, Charles I was found guilty of making war against his own people. On 30 January 1649 he was executed.

This picture shows the execution of Charles I. It was made by some of the king's supporters soon after he died. Can you see his soul rising up to heaven? The 'little god' has gone to be with God.

One last point: did you know that the little god was very little? Even as a grown man he was only 140 centimetres high – and that is including his head!

# Thinking your enquiry through

**There are lots of reasons why the English Civil War broke out. Some are shown in the boxes below. Historians have to find ways of sorting these reasons out.**

1 Sort the reasons into three groups as follows:

   Things to do with religion

   Things to do with money

   Things to do with power

2 Place the reasons on a **large** copy of this circle diagram. Use the overlaps for reasons which fit into more than one group.

3 You have sorted the reasons into three groups: Religion, Money and Power. However, there are lots of other ways of sorting the reasons out. Think of some other ways using different groups of your own, then make diagrams to see if your ideas work!

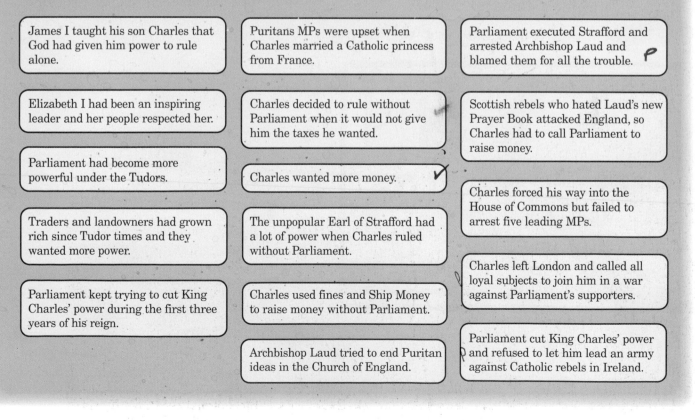

James I taught his son Charles that God had given him power to rule alone.

Puritans MPs were upset when Charles married a Catholic princess from France.

Parliament executed Strafford and arrested Archbishop Laud and blamed them for all the trouble. *P*

Elizabeth I had been an inspiring leader and her people respected her.

Charles decided to rule without Parliament when it would not give him the taxes he wanted.

Scottish rebels who hated Laud's new Prayer Book attacked England, so Charles had to call Parliament to raise money.

Parliament had become more powerful under the Tudors.

Charles wanted more money. ✓

Traders and landowners had grown rich since Tudor times and they wanted more power.

The unpopular Earl of Strafford had a lot of power when Charles ruled without Parliament.

Charles forced his way into the House of Commons but failed to arrest five leading MPs.

Parliament kept trying to cut King Charles' power during the first three years of his reign.

Charles used fines and Ship Money to raise money without Parliament.

Charles left London and called all loyal subjects to join him in a war against Parliament's supporters.

Archbishop Laud tried to end Puritan ideas in the Church of England.

Parliament cut King Charles' power and refused to let him lead an army against Catholic rebels in Ireland.

# 'The maddest world we ever saw'

## What made Britain seem so out of control between 1642 and 1660?

By 1647 the English Civil War had been going on for five years. Many people were shocked by what was happening. Here is the front cover of a booklet which was published in London at that time.

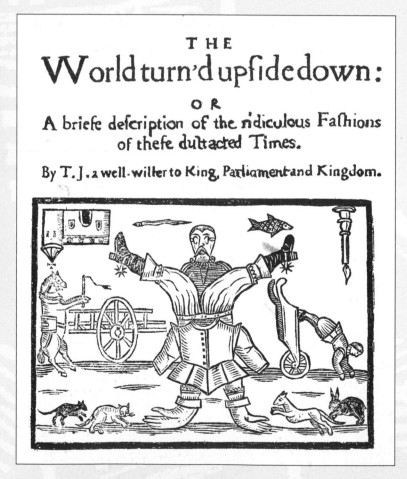

THE
World turn'd upside down:
OR
A briefe description of the ridiculous Fashions of these distracted Times.

By T. J. a well-willer to King, Parliament and Kingdom.

## Think

- Look at the picture. List all the ways in which the artist has shown an 'upside down world'?

- The writer is called T.J. Look at what he says about himself on the cover. Do you think he supports the king or Parliament or neither of them?

## Your enquiry

The booklet said that the world was upside down in 1647. In 1649 another writer thought things had grown even worse. He told a friend that Britain was 'the maddest world we ever saw'. By the end of this enquiry you will be able to explain why the world seemed 'mad' to so many people between 1642 and 1660.

# The 'madness' of the war

The war began in 1642. The king's supporters insulted Parliament's supporters by calling them '**Roundheads**'. This word was usually used to describe rough, short-haired young men who joined mobs in the towns. The Roundheads called the king's supporters '**Cavaliers**'. A Cavalier was a wild Spanish horseman. This cartoon from 1642 shows the war as a dog-fight between the two groups.

The country did not split neatly into two sides. Most great landowners supported the king – but some supported Parliament. Most merchants were Roundheads – but some were Cavaliers. Whole towns, counties and families were bitterly divided. People were often shocked and upset to find that close friends had become enemies.

It was a confusing world to live in. These maps show how the areas controlled by king and Parliament kept changing as the war progressed. They also show that the so-called **English** Civil War involved **Wales** and **Scotland**. The war spread to **Ireland** as well.

## Think

- Find the place where you live. Was it under the control of the Cavaliers (Royalists) or the Roundheads (Parliamentarians) in 1642?

- Which side seemed to be winning in 1643?

- Which side seemed to be winning in 1645?

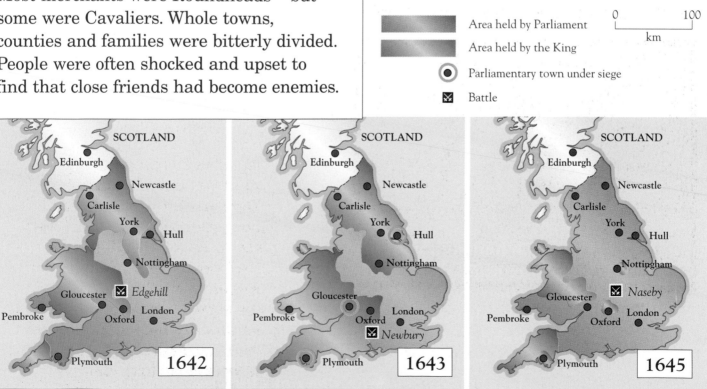

How the areas controlled by King and Parliament changed

Of course, many people did not want to get involved at all. They just wanted to get on with their normal lives. Some people refused to support either side. They formed their own armies of clubmen to keep the Roundhead and Cavalier armies out. But it was very difficult to avoid the dangers altogether.

The weapons you can see on this page give some idea of the injuries that must have been suffered in battles and ambushes. The muskets were usually fired at very close range and then used as clubs in hand-to-hand fighting. The pikes were heavy and clumsy. After a while the soldiers would drop them and fight with their swords. Men were pressed so closely together that those who were killed sometimes could not fall to the ground. Cannons fired into the closely-packed ranks of men and blew them to pieces.

*A modern reconstruction of the Battle of Marston Moor by the English Civil War Society*

When men ran away they were in great danger. One cavalry captain described how his men chased the enemy until their swords were blunted with the slaughter. The soldiers usually stripped any weapons, clothes or valuables from the dead and looted property from nearby houses. Roundheads often destroyed any statues, paintings or stained glass in local churches. War was not glorious.

Women were caught up in the war as well. A few women joined the fighting. Many more looked after the wounded and the sick. Some rich ladies organised the defence of their land and houses while their husbands were away. One poorer woman found fame by beating a soldier to death with the stick she had been using to stir the laundry. Thousands of women became widows and took their children and joined crippled soldiers begging in the cities.

*A print showing beggars during the English Civil War, made in 1647*

The Roundheads finally won the war. An important reason for this was that one of their generals, Oliver Cromwell, turned Parliament's soldiers into a well-disciplined fighting force. It became known as the 'New Model Army'. It trained hard and was paid regularly. Cromwell even used men from poor backgrounds as his captains, provided they had faith in God and were skilled in battle. At that time this was shocking. Only gentlemen and noblemen served as officers in the king's army.

In 1645 the New Model Army defeated Charles I at Naseby in Northamptonshire. By 1647 the king was captured. Whatever would happen next?

### STEP 1

Write a heading <u>The English Civil War shocked people because ...</u>
Underneath write a list of things about the war which must have shocked many people at that time. Use the section called 'The madness of the war' (pages 75 to 77) to help you. Make your list as long as you can.

# The 'madness' of the axe

It was strange to see the God-given king in captivity – but there were stranger things to come. In 1648, Charles persuaded his supporters in Scotland to start the war again. This was too much for people like Oliver Cromwell. He swiftly beat the Scottish army. Meanwhile other soldiers forced Parliament to put the king on trial for treason.

Many people who supported Parliament were worried. Did they have the right to try their king? People could commit **treason** against their king, but could a king commit treason against his people? The trial went ahead in January 1649. 135 men were appointed to try the king but only 68 turned up. Charles refused to accept that it was a true court and did not try to defend himself until it was too late. He was found guilty and was sentenced to death.

At 2pm on 30 January 1649 Charles rested his neck on the block at Whitehall in London. A few moments later the axe fell. The crowd groaned. It was as if they could not believe what they had seen – but there was no turning back now.

# The 'madness' of the dreamers

The king was dead. A new age had begun and some people began to dream of new ways of running the country. Here are three groups whose ideas seemed wild and dangerous to many other people at that time. (Many of their ideas seem very sensible to us now!)

## The Levellers

- Everyone over 21 (except women and servants) should be allowed to vote.
- Anyone may follow any religion.
- No one should be executed except for committing murder.
- Some women Levellers told Parliament that they should be allowed to vote. One cartoonist was so shocked that he drew this cartoon to show where he thought this idea would lead.

## The Quakers

- There is no need for organised church services.
- Women should be allowed to preach.
- Everyone is equal.
- Prisons should be less cruel.
- Violence is always wrong.
- No one should be spoken to with more respect than anyone else. (The father of one young Quaker was so upset when his son treated him like any other person that he threatened to 'strike his teeth down his throat'. The father was obviously not a Quaker.)

## The Diggers

- All the land must be shared out among the people.

The Quakers (or 'Friends') as they prefer to be called, still exist today. The other groups soon died away. Royalists hated them. Even men like Oliver Cromwell, who normally allowed Protestants a lot of freedom, could not put up with ideas like these. Like most people he believed that only men with property should hold power.

THE 1287
Parliament of Women:
With the merry Laws by them newly Enacted; To live in more Eafe, Pomp, Pride, and Wantonnefs: But efpecially that they might have Superiority, and domineer over their Husbands. With a new way found out by them to cure any old, or new Cuckolds, and how both parties may recover their credit and honefty again.

LONDON, Printed for W.W. and are to be fold by Fra.Grove, at his fhop on Snow-hill, near the Sarazens-head. 1656.

**STEP 2**

Write two new lists like the one you made in Step 1. Your headings this time are <u>The death of Charles I shocked people because ...</u> and <u>Levellers, Diggers and Quakers shocked people because ...</u>

# The 'madness' of the 'brave, bad man'

One name keeps appearing in this chapter: Oliver Cromwell. He was a Puritan MP from Cambridgeshire. He rose to fame as a general in Parliament's army. One of his enemies once called him a 'brave, bad man'. Between 1649 and 1658 he had more power than anyone else in Britain.

In 1649 Cromwell took the New Model Army to Ireland. All through the early years of the English Civil War he had been hearing dreadful stories from Protestants in Ireland. Here is an example:

> The Catholics commit horrible cruelties. They cut off people's private parts and their hands and feet. They dash out the brains of young children. They rip up women's bellies. They beat out their brains with poles.

*From a letter by Sir John Clotworthy, a Protestant landowner, December 1641*

No one knows whether the Catholics really did these things, but Cromwell certainly believed they did. As a Puritan, he believed that God wanted him to punish the Catholics. When Catholic rebels in the Irish town of Drogheda refused to surrender to his army he was in no mood to grant them mercy. He ordered his soldiers to kill all the rebel soldiers in the fort. When hundreds hid in the church, Cromwell told his men to set it on fire. Many were burnt alive. Every priest in the town was killed. Religious wars like this were common in Europe at that time. It seemed that Britain was sliding into the same sort of madness.

*A bust of Oliver Cromwell*

Once Ireland was under control, Cromwell returned to England. The New Model Army was soon in action again. Charles II (as Royalists now called the oldest son of the dead king) led a Scottish army against England. Cromwell beat him at Dunbar in 1650 and Worcester in 1651. Charles escaped and lived abroad for nine years before he was finally able to take the throne. In the meantime Oliver Cromwell seemed to become more and more like a king.

WITHAL

*A Dutch cartoon of Cromwell as king*

While Cromwell was at war he expected Parliament to be improving the country. MPs who supported Charles I had not been allowed into Parliament since 1648. The 60 MPs who were left had ended the monarchy and had turned Britain into a **republic** called the **Commonwealth**. But these MPs became greedy and unpopular. They let taxes rise and made themselves rich.

## In April 1653, Parliament had a sudden shock.

Cromwell took 30 soldiers to the House of Commons and threw the MPs out. In 1649 Charles I had taken soldiers to the House of Commons and sparked off the English Civil War. Now Cromwell, who had done so much to win the war for Parliament, was using the army to close Parliament down.

For the next five years Cromwell ran the country. He was called the Lord Protector. He tried all sorts of ways of sharing his power but none worked. People decided that the country needed a king after all. They offered the crown to Cromwell. He refused – but he accepted extra powers and agreed that his son would take over as Lord Protector when he died. This is what he said in 1656:

> I did not push myself into this position. I could not refuse the power God put into my hands.

His enemies said he was just greedy for power. They said that he had killed a king to become a king, in everything but name.

## Think

- Cromwell's enemies said that he was just greedy for power. What do you think his supporters might have said to defend him?

Cromwell allowed other Puritans to have a lot of power. They wanted to end all wicked behaviour. New laws closed all theatres because Puritans thought the Devil was at work there. Dancing around maypoles on May Day was banned. Many inns were shut down. Bull baiting and bear baiting were forbidden. (These were popular sports where people watched dogs attacking a bull or bear held in chains.) No one was allowed to work or even to play football on Sundays. This Puritan leaflet shows people how to use Sundays.

## Think

- Work out what Puritans liked people to do on Sundays. (Use the pictures down the left side of the illustration.)

- Work out what Puritans did not like people to do on Sundays. (Use the pictures down the right side of the illustration.)

Puritans made Christmas Day a day of fasting. No one was supposed to eat. Soldiers even went through London pulling meat from people's ovens! If anyone was caught swearing, they had to pay a fine. For many people these Puritans seemed to be making the 'maddest world' they ever saw.

When Cromwell died in 1658 his son, Richard, tried to take over as Lord Protector. He soon gave up. By 1660 even the Puritans and the army agreed that the country needed to invite Charles II back to rule as king. His supporters rejoiced. For them, the madness was over.

## STEP 3

Write another list like the ones you made in Steps 1 and 2. Use the heading <u>Oliver Cromwell shocked people because ...</u> Find lots of examples from the section called 'The madness of the brave, bad man' (pages 80 to 83).

# Thinking your enquiry through

In this enquiry you have seen cartoons that people made between 1642 and 1660. The cartoons **exaggerate** what really happened, but they show how shocked many people were at the time. Cartoons show us people's attitudes and opinions.

From the lists you have made in Steps 1, 2 and 3 choose one thing that really shocked people at the time that would be ideal for a cartoon. Draw your own cartoon as if it had been drawn by someone who was shocked. Remember that cartoons always **exaggerate** in order to make their point.

Your cartoon should be based upon one of the following:

- The English Civil War
- The execution of Charles 1
- The Levellers, Diggers and Quakers
- Oliver Cromwell's time in power

If you do not like drawing, write some instructions to a professional artist about what you want to appear in your cartoon.

# Monarchs in their place

## Who had control after 1660?

This is what is left of Oliver Cromwell's head. He died on 3 September 1658. His body was preserved in spices. For ten weeks people flocked to London to see his corpse. On 23 November 1658 he was given one of the biggest funerals the city had ever seen. It cost over two million pounds. Thirty thousand soldiers lined the streets to Westminster Abbey.

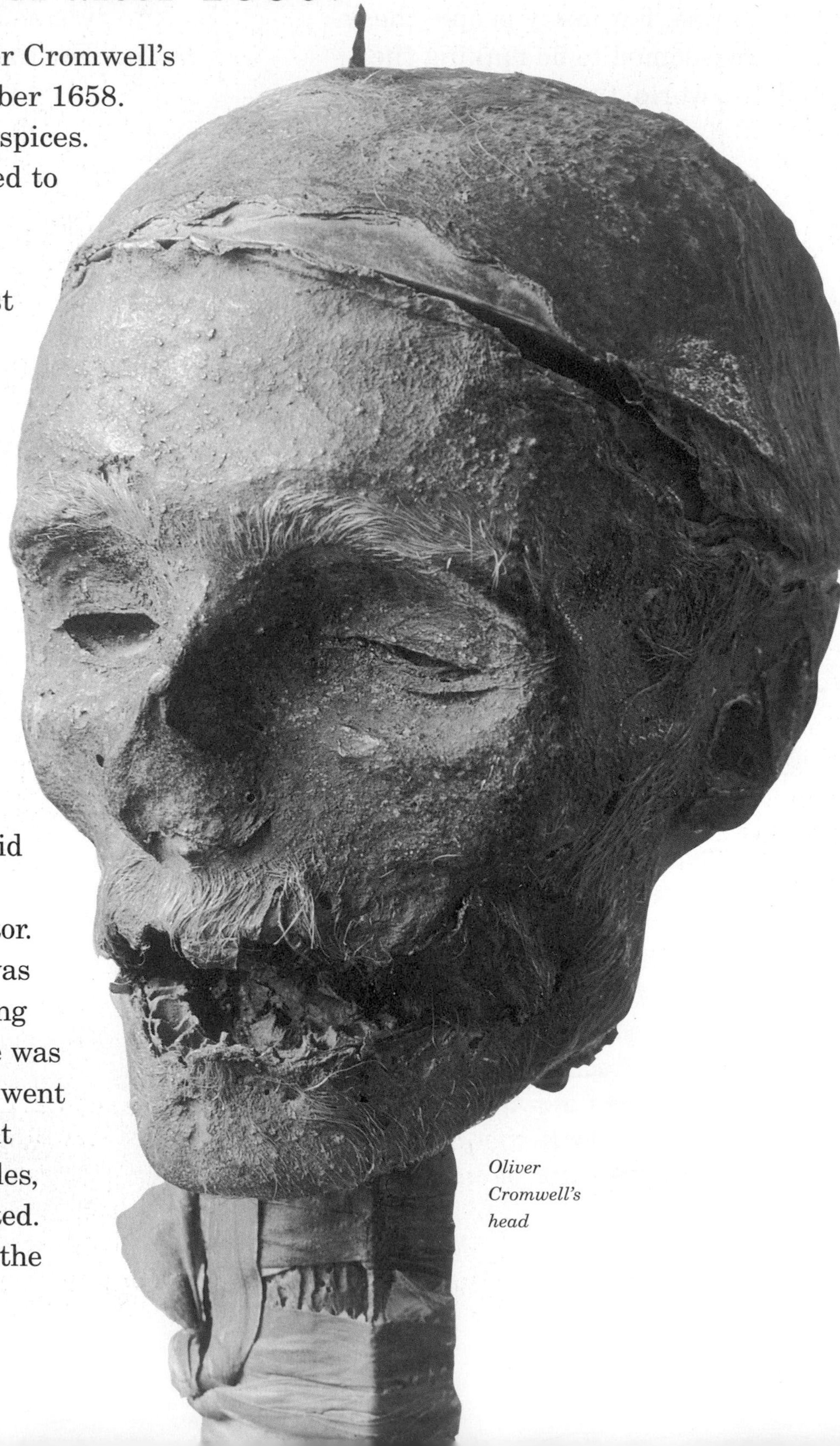

Before he died Cromwell said that his elder son, Richard, should become Lord Protector. Richard was a farmer. He was not really interested in ruling his country. In May 1659 he was forced out by the army and went back to his farm. Parliament asked Charles I's son, Charles, to return as king. He accepted. The Republic was over and the monarchy was restored.

*Oliver Cromwell's head*

84

*The coronation procession of Charles II*

This picture shows Charles II returning to England. Many of the people who had lined the streets for Cromwell's funeral now cheered at the sight of their new king. Within weeks Cromwell's corpse had been dug up and hanged. His head was stuck on a pole at the corner of Westminster Hall. It blew down in a gale one night and someone stole it. Many years later it was buried at Cambridge University, where Cromwell had been a student.

## Your enquiry

Cromwell was dead and buried (for a short time!). The monarchy was restored. But how powerful were the monarchs who ruled after 1660? In this enquiry you will decide whether the kings and queens were still in charge or whether they were put in their place. Over the next few pages six monarchs explain what happened during their reigns.

# Charles II  1660–1685

❝ Ever since my father was executed in 1649, I had waited for the day when I could return to England. My chance came in 1660. Parliament wanted a monarch again and they offered me the crown. The Republic was over. I took my rightful place on the English throne.

Parliament gave me all the powers which my father had enjoyed. They allowed me to choose my **ministers** and to control my own army. If only they had given me enough money as well. How could I rule with a treasury that was half empty?

My biggest quarrel with Parliament was about religion. I was a Catholic, but kept this a secret until the day I died. I had hoped that all my subjects would be allowed to worship freely, but Parliament would not allow this. They wanted to punish anyone who was not a member of the Church of England.

I had 13 children altogether. None of them could rule after me because they were all **illegitimate**. Parliament was afraid that the throne would pass to my Catholic brother James. In 1679 they even tried to pass a law which stopped any Catholic becoming king.

**I was furious** and made sure that they did not succeed. For the last four years of my reign I ruled without Parliament. How dare they try to stop my brother James from **inheriting** the throne! ❞

*King Charles II*

86

# James II  *1685–1688*

**"** Everything seemed so good when I took over from my brother Charles in 1685. Parliament gave me enough money and I was able to build up a large army. Imagine how angry I was when the Duke of Monmouth, a bastard son of Charles II, landed in England and tried to overthrow me. Few of my people supported him. I had the rebels' bodies cut into quarters, salted and displayed in the towns of the south west of England.

I did not hide my Catholicism like my brother had done. I made sure that Catholics were given important jobs in the government and army. When my ministers disagreed with me I sacked them. When Parliament was a nuisance I sent it away and made my own laws.

*James II*

Many of the leading politicians hoped that my Protestant daughter, Mary, would become queen when I died. They were furious when my wife gave birth to a baby son. You see, they thought the boy would follow in my footsteps by ruling as a true Catholic. That is why these evil men secretly invited Mary's husband, William of Orange, to invade England in the summer of 1688. This time my people did not support me.

I had a nervous breakdown and escaped to France in the middle of the night. William had stolen my kingdom from me. I had ruled for only three years. They called this the Glorious Revolution.

## The fools! **"**

### STEP 1

Make a chart like this one. Put in as much information as you can about Charles II and James II.

|  | Still in charge | Losing power |
|---|---|---|
| Charles II |  |  |
| James II |  |  |

# William and Mary 1688–1702

*William III*

**"** Invading England in 1688 was a risk, but it worked. I refused to let my wife Mary rule alone. So Parliament invited us to become joint rulers. Unfortunately Parliament also passed a Bill of Rights in 1689 which limited our power. They were determined not to give me the powers which Charles II and James II had enjoyed. I was never allowed to rule without Parliament. I always had to obey Parliament's laws. I could not raise taxes by myself or keep my own army.

At first I was popular in England, but those Irish Catholics hated me. The wicked traitors formed an army to support James II when he tried to take back the throne in 1690. I went to Ireland myself at the head of my English and Dutch army. We slaughtered the Catholics at the Battle of the Boyne. James was defeated and scurried off to France again.

For most of my reign I got on well with Parliament. I still made important decisions. I worked late into the night to make sure that I was in control. The long and bitter war against the French took up most of my time. Fortunately, Parliament gave me the money I needed to fight the war.

My wife died in 1694 and I ruled alone until 1702, when I broke my collar bone trying out a new horse in Richmond Park. I died of a chill shortly after. Mary and I had no children and the throne passed to my wife's sister, Anne. **"**

# Anne 1702–1714

*Queen Anne*

**66** When I inherited the throne in 1702 I was 37. I had been pregnant eighteen times, but only five of my babies were born alive and all of these died as children. Some people say I was not as clever or as interested in ruling as William III, but I wonder how strong **he** would have been after eighteen pregnancies!

My main interests were playing dominoes and drinking brandy. I relied on my close friends to run the country. People called them my 'managers'. They had a lot of power, but if I did not like the way they did things I sacked them. During my reign Parliament took away no more of the monarch's powers. But I never dared to dismiss Parliament as my father, James II, had done.

I was the first British monarch to see a single Parliament for both England and Scotland. In 1707, the Act of Union joined England and Scotland together as one country. Many Scots were unhappy with this. They wanted to have a separate country and their own monarch. When I died in 1714 Parliament decided that the throne should pass to my nearest Protestant heir, George, Elector of Hanover. **99**

## STEP 2

**Add more information to the chart you began in Step 1. Put in as many points as you can about William III and Anne.**

# George I 1714–1727

“ At first I was not sure that I wanted the British throne. In Hanover I was in control and did not have to consult a parliament. Ruling Britain was not going to be as easy. Look what happened to Charles I and James II! I spoke very little English and was not very interested in Britain. I went back to Hanover as often as I could.

I left the government in the hands of my ministers. The most important of these men was Robert Walpole. He had the support of Parliament and no one really challenged him during his 21 years in office. Some people have called him Britain's first Prime Minister. This did not mean that I had no power. It was the king's right to choose his ministers. Walpole only survived for so long because I liked his policies. When I died in 1727 I left a secure throne. Britain was a peaceful and wealthy country. Not that **my dreadful son** deserved it! ”

*George I*

# George II 1727–1760

*George II*

“ How I **hated my father!** He locked up my mother for having a boyfriend and never allowed me to see her. I never forgave him. I detested Walpole too, but he promised me a lot of money so I kept him on. Lots of people thought he had too much power. They began to produce rude cartoons like this one.

Walpole finally resigned in 1742. I was forced to take on William Pitt whom I detested even more. Other ministers were chosen by Parliament against my wishes. I kicked my coat and wig about in a terrible rage.

My biggest scare came in 1745. 'Bonnie Prince Charlie', grandson of James II, landed in Scotland and tried to force me off the throne. My army slaughtered the Jacobites at the Battle of Culloden. The Stuarts never again tried to win back the crown and I ruled for another 15 years. ”

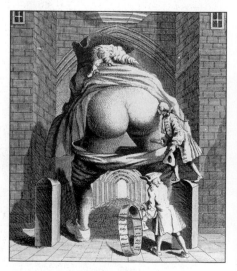

*Cartoon of politicians kissing Sir Robert Walpole's bottom*

Add the final information to your chart. Put in as much information as you can about George I and George II.

# Thinking your enquiry through

A balloon debate

Imagine a silly situation. Our six monarchs are in a balloon together. The balloon is losing air. Three monarchs will have to jump out. These should be the three who have lost most power.

You need to work in seven groups. Six of the groups will each defend one monarch. One group will be the judges.

If your group is defending a monarch use the information in your chart to persuade the judges that your monarch should stay in the balloon and to criticise one of the other monarchs. Collect as many ideas as you can.

If you are in the group of judges you need to use the information in your chart to begin deciding who should go. Remember that you will not be able to make your final decision until you have heard all the evidence.

When you are prepared, hold your balloon debate and make your decisions.

# Forcing minds to change

## 1547 to 1603: When was it most dangerous to speak your mind?

This painting is called 'Man of Sorrows'. It was painted in the northern Netherlands during the 1520s. It is meant to be sad and disturbing.

*Christ, Man of Sorrows, painted in the Netherlands in about 1525*

All over Europe, paintings like this helped Christians to think about the death of Jesus Christ.

## Think

- How has the artist created a feeling of sorrow and suffering? Find all the details which show this.

- Why do you think that the artist has put angels in the painting?

The painting below was also painted in the Netherlands, but over a hundred years later. Like the first painting, it shows us that Christianity was still terribly important – just as important as it had been a hundred years before.

However, by the time this picture was painted, something had happened. An enormous change had taken place. Christians in Europe had split into two camps: Catholics and Protestants.

You can see the hand of God at the top of the painting. God is weighing the beliefs of Protestants and Catholics in weighing scales. On the left are the Catholics and on the right are the Protestants.

*A Dutch painting from the early seventeenth century*

The painting is designed to persuade people that the Protestants are right. However, people at this time did not always rely on persuasion. If persuasion did not work, each side was prepared to use **force**.

## Think

● How does the painter show that he supports the Protestants?

## Your enquiry

These were dangerous times all over Europe. Changes in religion were happening so quickly that it was hard to keep up. Catholics and Protestants could be punished and even put to death for sticking to the wrong set of beliefs at the wrong time. You are going to work out where and when it was dangerous for different types of Christians in England and Wales. At the end of the enquiry you will produce a guide to the dangers – your own Danger Chart.

# Making the changes 1

## The protestant reformers

In the early sixteenth century many people were criticising the Roman Catholic Church. Soon, huge changes were taking place. Europe had never seen anything like it before.

Of course, many people had been criticising the Roman Catholic Church for some time. There was nothing new in that. But now some very inspiring leaders started to gain large followings. These leaders are called reformers. The changes are called the **Reformation**. Two of the most important reformers were Martin Luther and John Calvin. People who followed Luther and Calvin were protesting about what they thought was wrong with the Church. The things that Luther and Calvin taught were very shocking. The Roman Catholic Church taught that priests were necessary to find God and that the only head of the Church was the Pope.

### Think

- Why were Martin Luther and John Calvin called 'reformers'?

- Why were the people who followed them named 'protestants'?

**Martin Luther** began his protest against the Roman Catholic Church in Germany in 1517. Here are some of the things that he taught.

**John Calvin** spread his new ideas in Switzerland in the 1530s. He went even further than Luther. His ideas were more extreme. Here are some of the things that he taught.

Believing in Jesus Christ is the only way to gain God's forgiveness.

Believing in Jesus Christ is more important than going to Mass or making pilgrimages.

Ordinary people should read the Bible for themselves, in their own language.

Ordinary people do not need priests to find God.

The ruler of each country should be head of the Church, not the Pope.

Church services should be very simple: no crosses, candles, pictures or robes.

The bread and wine are just symbols. They do not change into Jesus' body and blood.

Ordinary people should read the Bible for themselves, in their own language.

There should be no priests at all. Members of each congregation should elect their own minister or 'presbyter'.

94

# Making the changes 2

## Kings and queens

The ideas of the reformers soon spread to other countries. Some kings and queens in Europe liked the reformers' ideas. Others did not. It was not long before the reformers' ideas reached Britain.

## In England and Wales:

## Edward VI 1547–1553

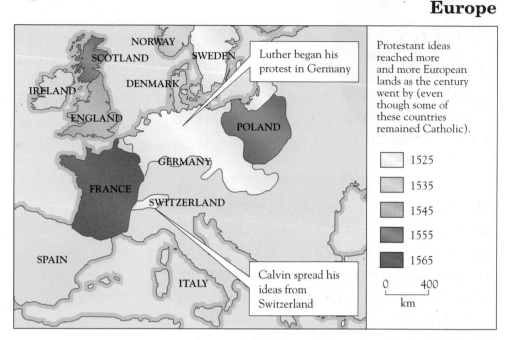

Luther began his protest in Germany

Calvin spread his ideas from Switzerland

Protestant ideas reached more and more European lands as the century went by (even though some of these countries remained Catholic).

- 1525
- 1535
- 1545
- 1555
- 1565

0        400
km

Edward VI was only nine when he became king. He and all his advisers were strongly **Protestant**. They began to create a Protestant church. Priests were told to wear simple, white linen garments, instead of their usual fancy **vestments**. Priests had to replace stone altars with wooden **communion** tables. In 1549, a new Prayer Book was written by the archbishop, Thomas Cranmer. It was in English. In his second Prayer Book of 1552 an astonishing change was made. The old Catholic Mass was replaced by a much simpler 'communion' service.

There were no executions, although one Catholic bishop was imprisoned for opposing the changes. Bishops who clung to the old ways were replaced. Protestant preachers worked hard to persuade people to accept the changes, but some people carried on worshipping peacefully in the old ways. In Lancashire, many Catholic communities managed to avoid the changes altogether.

### Meanwhile in Scotland:

Here the ideas of John Calvin spread rapidly. In 1560 the Scottish Parliament set up a special Protestant church called a **Presbyterian** church. In 1567, Mary, Queen of Scots, a Catholic, was forced to give up her throne to her Protestant son, James.

95

## Mary I 1553–1558

Mary was a **Roman Catholic**. She changed everything back again! The Pope was restored as head of the English Church. All the changes made by Edward VI were cancelled. Services were once again held in Latin. In 1554 Mary married a Roman Catholic, Philip of Spain. She also began to **persecute** the Protestants. During her reign about three hundred Protestants were burned to death. One of these people was Thomas Cranmer, the archbishop who rewrote the Prayer Book in Edward's reign.

Now let me see … Whose reign am I in? What should the church look like?

**A Catholic church during the reign of Mary I**

**A Protestant church during the reign of Edward VI**

# Coping with the changes

## Ordinary lives

All over Europe ordinary people were caught up in the changes. Ordinary people did not always hold the same beliefs as their rulers. Sometimes people changed their minds freely. Sometimes they were forced to change their minds. Sometimes they fled to other countries where they hoped to be safer.

During Mary's reign it was dangerous to be a Protestant. Some very famous and important people like the former archbishop, Thomas Cranmer, were burnt at the stake, but most of the people burnt in Mary's reign were ordinary people. Here is a list of all the people who were burnt:

## MEN

| | |
|---|---|
| 21 priests | 2 tailors, butchers, smiths, bricklayers, carpenters, servants |
| 13 weavers | |
| 9 gentlemen | 1 apothecary, schoolmaster, merchant, linen-draper. |
| 7 husbandmen | |
| 6 labourers | 1 constable, cook, barber, glazier, artificer, wheelwright, glover, shoemaker, miller, merchant |
| 4 fullers, shearmen | |
| 3 tanners, sawyers, brewers, painters | 114 unknown |

## WOMEN

| | |
|---|---|
| 6 widows | 2 wives of millers |
| 25 wives | 2 wives of weavers |
| 5 unmarried | 1 wife of a brewer, a pewterer, a shoemaker, an upholsterer |
| 1 gentlewoman | |
| 5 wives of husbandmen | 1 blind daughter of a ropemaker |
| 2 servant maids | 19 unknown |

*Statistics of martyrs, taken from P Hughes 'The Reformation in England', 1950*

We know quite a lot about some of these people because their stories are recorded in the 'Book of **Martyrs**' by John Foxe.

John Foxe was a Protestant. In his book he made all Catholics appear wicked and cruel. He wanted his readers to remember the courage and faith of the Protestants. Here is a picture from Foxe's book. It shows four people being burnt to death for their beliefs.

## Think

- Why do you think that so many Protestants were prepared to be burnt to death rather than change their faith?
- Why did John Foxe write this book?
- Why should historians be very careful when using the stories in Foxe's book?

## STEP 1

**Look carefully at the information about the reigns of Edward and Mary. Decide how much danger you think each religious group was in during the different reigns. Make a table like the one below. In the middle column write a number from 1 to 5 to show the level of danger (1 = very safe, 5 = very dangerous). In the last column explain why you chose the number.**

| | Danger scale 1–5 | Explanation |
|---|---|---|
| Protestants in Edward VI's reign | | |
| Catholics in Edward VI's reign | | |
| Protestants in Mary's reign | | |
| Catholics in Mary's reign | | |

# Queen Elizabeth I

## A church for everyone?

Mary gained the nickname Bloody Mary because of her persecution of the Protestants during her reign. This is probably very unfair. She was cruel by modern standards, but so were other rulers. Henry VIII was always executing people for disagreeing with him. Mary's half-sister, Elizabeth, could be very cruel too. She persecuted **both** Catholics **and** some Protestants! She executed many people during her reign.

Queen Elizabeth was a Protestant, but she wanted to bring peace and order to the land after all the bloodshed and hatred. She thought that the best way to do this was to find a Church with which everyone would be happy. In 1559 she created a Protestant Church.

Once again there was an English prayer book. Once again there was an English bible. Soon there was a Welsh prayer book and a Welsh bible too.

However, this was a much gentler kind of Protestantism than Edward's. Elizabeth did not like the extreme ideas of John Calvin. She preferred the more moderate Protestantism of Luther. She wanted a Protestantism which was still very similar to the Catholic Church. **Elizabeth was trying to find a middle way.**

The trouble was, that this made her all the more angry with anyone who tried to spoil her middle way!

**Puritans** wanted the Church to be even more Protestant. Elizabeth would not listen to them.

**Roman Catholics** wanted to worship freely. Elizabeth controlled and sometimes persecuted them.

# Puritans

Extreme Protestants (or Puritans) caused more and more problems for Elizabeth. She started to get very tough on them during the 1580s. Puritans believed that ordinary people could get in touch with God by reading the Bible and leading a pure, simple life. They believed that priests had too much power. The Puritans thought that churches should not be run by bishops appointed by the monarch, but by ministers elected by church members.

Puritans disapproved of playing sports and games. They did not like music in church services. Many of them followed the ideas of John Calvin of Geneva. There were all sorts of stories about Calvin's strict rules in Geneva. It was said that children were beaten if they were caught eating cakes on Sundays.

Here is a woodcut of a Puritan family during the time of Elizabeth.

Puritans were free to get on with their lives, but if they spoke out, Elizabeth could be very harsh. She had a lot of trouble with Puritans in Parliament who tried to tell her that her church was not Protestant enough. This made her unbelievably angry. For Elizabeth, the whole point was to find a church to which everyone could belong.

In 1583 she took action against a Puritan who wrote a book which she did not like. This account was written shortly after her reign, in 1615, by someone who witnessed the event:

From this time on, Elizabeth became a little more angry with the Puritans. John Stubbs was sentenced to have his right hand cut off with cleaver, driven through the wrist with the force of a mallet, upon a scaffold in the market place at Westminster ... I remember (being present at the time) that Stubbs, after his right hand was cut off, took off his hat with his left hand, and said with a loud voice, 'God save the Queen!'

## Think

- Elizabeth I was not too bothered about Puritans choosing to live plain and simple lives. Which of their ideas do you think annoyed her a great deal?

# Catholics

Even though England was now a Protestant country, many Catholic families carried on living there. It was easier for rich Catholic families to go on avoiding Protestantism. They could afford to pay the weekly fine for not going to church.

However, it was very difficult for them to worship. Priests were very important to Catholics. Elizabeth knew this. Keeping priests out of the country was the best way of controlling Catholics. When there were plots to put a Catholic monarch on the throne, she began to persecute Catholic priests and anyone who protected them.

From the 1580s things became very difficult for Catholics. Elizabeth feared that they would plot with the Spanish against her.

This picture shows a hiding place under the floor boards in a country house belonging to a rich Catholic family. If the soldiers came, the priest got inside quickly.

One Catholic priest called Edmund Campion was caught hiding in a house after saying Mass. Whilst in prison he suffered many cruel tortures. Iron spikes were driven under his fingernails and toenails.

Here is an account of his execution:

They called to him to pray in English, but he replied with great mildness that he would pray to God in a language which they both well understood. There was more noise. The councillors demanded that he should ask the Queen's forgiveness. Wherein have I offended her? In this I am innocent. This is my last speech. In this give me credit: I have and do pray for her.

The cart was then driven from under him, the eager crowd swayed forward, and Campion was left hanging, until, unconscious, perhaps already dead, he was cut down and the butcher began his work.

## Think
- Work out *how* Campion was executed.
- Explain *why* Campion was executed.

Using a danger scale of 1 to 5 (1 = very safe, 5 = very dangerous) decide how much danger you think each religious group was in during Elizabeth's reign.

Make a table like the one below. In the middle column write a number from 1 to 5 to show the level of danger. In the last column explain why you chose the number.

| | Danger scale 1–5 | Explanation |
|---|---|---|
| Protestants | | |
| Puritans | | |
| Catholics | | |

# Thinking your enquiry through

To make your <u>Danger Chart</u> do the following:

1 Make a very big copy of this timeline:

**Catholic**  **Protestant**

Edward VI
1547–1553

Mary I
1553–1558

Elizabeth I
1558–1603

2 On each side write short 'danger guides' in little boxes.

In each box write a brief guide on the level of danger for Catholics or Protestants in each reign. Here are some sample danger guides. Work out where they belong and use them to start your chart:

### Danger guide
A very bad time to be a Catholic. If you are rich you may be all right. Just pay a weekly fine and keep quiet. Whatever you do, don't hide any priests!

### Danger guide
A good time if you are a fairly ordinary Protestant. It's safe to be a Puritan, but whatever you do, don't criticise the Church publicly for not being Puritan enough! If you do, say goodbye to your freedom (or to your right hand).

# Culture clash

## 12

## Why was there no meeting of minds in the New World?

*William Penn's Treaty with the Indians, 1681, painted in 1771*

This painting shows an important meeting which took place in 1681. The people on the left are English **settlers** in America. The people on the right are Native Americans.

## Think

- What are the settlers offering the Native Americans?

- What do you think they wanted in return?

102

# A New World

In 1492, an Italian sailor called Christopher Columbus arrived in a 'New World' – America. Columbus thought he had found a shorter route to the East. He called the people he found in America 'Indians'. About a hundred years later, many people from different European countries began to settle in America. We call these people **colonists**. The lands they settled are called **colonies**.

For the people who lived in America already, this was not a 'New World'. They had lived there for thousands of years. These Native Americans must have been very shocked when the first white people arrived on their shores. The Europeans spoke a strange language. They looked very odd with their white skins and peculiar clothes. They had unusual ways of doing things. Their **culture** was very different from the Native American way of life. At first the two groups of people traded peacefully. They exchanged metal tools and woven cloth for beaver skins and other furs. But before long the two cultures clashed.

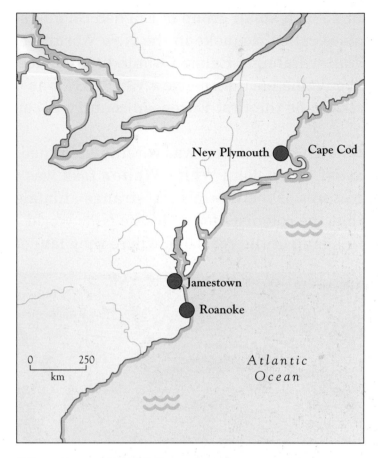

**The first English colonies in North America**

The colonists brought new diseases like measles and smallpox. They were greedy for land. Their guns enabled them to take the land from the Native Americans.

## Your enquiry

In this enquiry you will find out about the first three English colonies in the New World – Roanoke, Virginia and New Plymouth. You will work out why the white colonists clashed with the Native Americans. At the end of your enquiry you will explain why there was no meeting of minds in the New World.

# The first colony: Roanoke

In 1585, a small group of English colonists tried to settle at a place called Roanoke in the New World. They had been sent by Walter Raleigh. Raleigh wanted to find out as much as he could about this part of the New World. He was determined that England should be the first European country to colonise North America.

Raleigh's expedition was carefully planned. He even sent an artist called John White. White's task was to draw accurate pictures of the new plants, strange animals and puzzling people that the colonists found in the New World. He began by making this map of the coastline where they landed.

John White's map of the coast at Roanoke, 1585

## Think

● What dangers did the English colonists face?

● What clues are there on the map that this might have been a good place to live?

The Native Americans who lived in this part of the New World were called the Algonquin. John White made friends with them and made some very careful paintings of their way of life.

This picture shows one of their villages.

Life in an Algonquin village was very different from life in Europe. Native Americans believed that the land could not be owned by individual people. The land was part of nature and was for everyone to share. It could not be sold or fenced-off into little parcels. Native Americans believed in sharing the things they owned.

In an Algonquin village, people did not hunt just for themselves, but for the whole village. No one was allowed to go hungry if there was food to share.

*John White's painting of an Algonquin village*

## Think

- What do you think the colonists found strange about the Native Americans?

- What do you think the Native Americans found strange about the colonists?

them maize. When the Algonquin refused, the two groups began to quarrel. Things were starting to go wrong. Soon they were fighting. In the end the English colonists were forced to leave. The first English colony in the New World had failed.

At first the English colonists at Roanoke were on good terms with the Algonquin. The Algonquin showed the colonists how to plant maize. They exchanged animal skins for glasses, knives and cooking pots. Two Algonquin even went back to England to meet Elizabeth I!

Peace did not last for very long. Soon a hundred English soldiers came to Roanoke. They built a fort and started to take over the land. They forced the Algonquin to give

### STEP 1

**Use the introduction to this enquiry and the story of the first colony at Roanoke to answer the following questions:**

1 Why did the colonists go to the New World?

2 What did they do when they got there?

3 Why did they clash with the Native Americans?

# The second colony: Virginia

In April 1607, three small ships dropped anchor in Chesapeake Bay. The 105 people who had survived the difficult journey from London were a mixture of sailors, adventurers, poor farmers, gentlemen and criminals. These new colonists were hoping to find gold and silver in the New World.

As the colonists stepped onto dry land their legs felt shaky after four months at sea. They noticed Native Americans in the forest. Some of them had read stories which made them frightened of the native people. The colonists expected trouble. They quickly chopped down trees to build houses. The colonists called their settlement Jamestown after their king in England. They surrounded their settlement with a wooden stockade to protect themselves from attack by the Native Americans.

*A reconstruction of the fort at Jamestown*

The colonists managed to survive their first few months in the New World, but they soon used up their supplies. They began to steal food from the Native Americans. The colonists became weak. Many caught malaria and died. After two years there were only 38 people left in Jamestown.

Then several things happened which saved the colony:

1  Another ship brought new supplies and more colonists from England.

2  The colony found a strong leader, John Smith. He made everyone work hard.

3  One of the settlers, John Rolfe, married Pocahontas, daughter of the Native American chief in the area. Attacks by Native Americans stopped.

4  The Native Americans gave the colonists a strange weed which looked like dandelion. It was tobacco. King James hated it, but people in England loved it.

The colony grew stronger. More and more people arrived from England. All along the banks of the Chesapeake river colonists set up plantations. These plantations produced only one thing – tobacco. The Native Americans of the Chesapeake knew that they could not survive if they lost their hunting grounds. In 1622 they decided to fight back.

When their leader was murdered by the colonists the Native Americans attacked the English settlements. A third of the colonists were killed. After the war of 1622 John Smith said that the colonists now had a reason to destroy the Native Americans.

STEP 2

Use the story of the second colony at Virginia to answer the following questions:

1  Why did the colonists go to the New World?

2  What did they do when they got there?

3  Why did they clash with the Native Americans?

## Think

● How do you think each of these four things helped to save the colony?

# The third colony: New Plymouth

In September 1620, 101 men, women and children squashed on board a small ship called the 'Mayflower'. Nearly half the people on board were Puritans. In 1603, when James VI of Scotland became King of England, he had told the Puritans:

> You must obey me or I will chase you from this land, or else do worse.

He did not say what 'do worse' might mean. But many Puritans did not wait to find out. They decided that it was time to give up on England and to build their own godly community in a new land. At first they settled in the Netherlands, but in 1620 a small group sailed to the New World.

The Puritans and other colonists on the 'Mayflower' had a stormy journey across the Atlantic. They wanted to go to Virginia, but the ship was blown off course and eventually landed at Cape Cod. This picture shows the Puritans as they landed in America.

It was the middle of winter. The colonists were forced to build their houses while the snow was falling. Before spring came they had built some small log cabins, but half the colonists had died of cold or disease. The ones who survived now faced a new problem – hunger.

They were saved by a Native American called Squanto who had learnt to speak English from the colonists at Jamestown. Squanto showed the settlers at New Plymouth how to plant maize. The colonists began to hunt animals in the woods and fish for lobsters in the sea. They also started to buy furs from the Native Americans. By the autumn of 1621 the colony at New Plymouth was secure. To celebrate their success the colonists held a huge feast. They invited the Native Americans to celebrate with them.

Good relations with the Native Americans did not last long. The Puritans thought that they were chosen by God to farm the land in the New World. One Puritan described the Native Americans as '… only savage and brutish men, just like wild beasts'. The Puritans felt that the Native Americans did not use the land properly. The colonists began to put up fences and to take land away from the Native Americans.

The idea of dividing up the land seemed very strange to the Native Americans. For hundreds of years they had lived in harmony with the world around them. Now the white colonists were destroying this world with their fences, guns and diseases.

In 1622, trouble broke out when a group of new colonists arrived from England. The colonists stole maize from the Native Americans and killed their leader. They cut off his head and stuck it on top of the fort at New Plymouth. The cultures had clashed. The peace had ended.

STEP 3

Use the story of the third colony at New Plymouth to answer the following questions:

1 Why did the colonists go to the New World?

2 What did they do when they got there?

3 Why did they clash with the Native Americans?

# Thinking your enquiry through

The picture below shows a Native American and a colonist. They are face to face, but there is no meeting of minds. Draw an outline picture of the two faces, and beneath each one show all the things which explain why the two cultures did not live peacefully together in the New World. The list has been started for you.

Native Americans
People cannot own the land.

Colonists
We want to farm the land.

# Evil on their minds

## 13

## Why did people believe in witches?

This is a seventeenth-century painting of witches making contact with the Devil at a witches' meeting.

## Think

- Which people in the painting are the witches?

- What are they doing?

- What strange creatures can you see?

- Why might these strange creatures be there?

## Your enquiry

The painting seems very strange today, but the artist who painted it was not mad. In the seventeenth century almost everyone in Europe believed that a world of strange creatures overlapped with their own, everyday world. This evil world was controlled by the Devil. Witches were the Devil's helpers. People believed in witches during the Middle Ages, but during the sixteenth and seventeenth centuries Europe was gripped by a <u>witch-craze</u>. Thousands of women were hanged or burnt to death because people believed that they were witches. In this enquiry you will try to explain why **so many** intelligent and sensible people believed that witches existed.

# Witchcraft and the law

This picture is taken from a book about witchcraft written in the 1650s. It shows some witches being executed.

*Execution of witches in 1655*

## Think

- What are all the people in the picture doing?

- Why did people go to watch witches being executed?

- Why do you think witches were punished so harshly?

During the Middle Ages witches were put on trial in the Church courts, but the punishments were light and they were never put to death. In fact, very few witches were punished at all. It was during the reigns of the Tudor and Stuart monarchs that harsh laws were passed against witchcraft.

### During Henry VIII's reign (1509–1547)

*Henry VIII*

Henry VIII suspected that witches were involved in plots to kill him. In 1542 a law was passed which stated that witches should be punished by death. This law ended when Henry died in 1547.

### During Elizabeth I's reign (1558–1603)

*Elizabeth I*

Protestants persuaded Elizabeth I that tougher laws against witches were needed. In 1563 a new law was passed which brought back the death penalty for any witch who used magic to kill someone. Witches who harmed people were put in prison.

### During James I's reign (1603–1625)

*James I*

Some of James I's ministers were strict Puritans and they persuaded the king to introduce an even harsher law against witches. From 1604 anyone who was shown to have contacted evil spirits could be hanged for witchcraft, whether or not they had done any harm.

**STEP 1**

**Use the information in the section called 'Witchcraft and the law' (pages 111 to 112) to start to make a list of reasons why people might have believed in witches. Write four reasons. Use these words to help you:**

**Books   Laws   Executions   Monarchs**

# The witch-craze

It is difficult to say how many witches were executed under these harsh laws because very few court records have survived outside the south east of England. One historian has estimated that the total number of witches executed in England was probably less than one thousand. This was far fewer than in Scotland or in other European countries. There are two puzzling features of the English witch-craze. Both of them could help to explain why people believed in witches, so think about them carefully.

## The first puzzling feature ...

There seem to have been more witchcraft trials in years when people were living through times of great hardship or upheaval. In the 1580s and 1590s (a time of poor harvests, famine and rebellion) the number of witchcraft trials went up dramatically. During the English Civil War (1642–1649) witch-fever broke out again, particularly in those areas controlled by the Puritans.

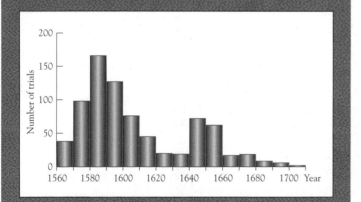

**Graph showing the number of witchcraft trials in South East England, 1560–1709**

## The second puzzling feature ...

Some parts of England had many more witchcraft trials than others. In the years between 1560 and 1701, for example, there were only 16 witchcraft trials in Sussex. Essex had 279. Essex was a strong Puritan area. In many villages there was a lot of tension between rich and poor people during the seventeenth century.

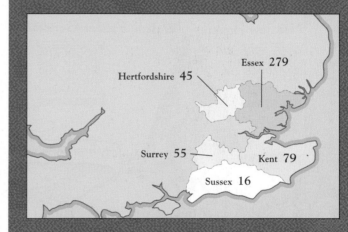

**Map showing the number of witchcraft trials in South East England, 1560–1701**

## Think

- When were there most witchcraft trials?
- Name one county where the number of witchcraft trials was remarkably high.
- Why did the number of witchcraft trials vary so much?

## STEP 2

You should now be able to think of two or three more reasons why so many people believed witches existed. Add them to the list you began in Step 1.

# The Black Art

Before we can produce a good explanation of why so many people believed witches existed, we need to understand how people thought witches worked and why people were so afraid of them.

People believed that witches obtained their evil power by meeting the Devil in person at a Sabbath. The Devil gave the witches evil powers to use during their lifetime in return for their souls when they died. After worshipping the Devil at a Sabbath witches were given a familiar – an evil spirit which often took the form of a small animal.

There are several familiars shown in this picture of Matthew Hopkins, a famous witch-finder.

People believed that the witch fed her familiars on her own blood. A witch would have a witch-mark on her body, such as a wart or mole, and this was where the familiar sucked her blood.

## Think

- What names have the familiars in the picture been given?
- Which of these animals look like ordinary pets?

Matthew Hopkins, Witch-finder General, questioning a witch
A seventeenth-century illustration

Very few people who were brought to trial for witchcraft in England were accused of attending a Sabbath or of worshipping the Devil. Here are some examples from witchcraft trials of the kind of accusations that people made against witches:

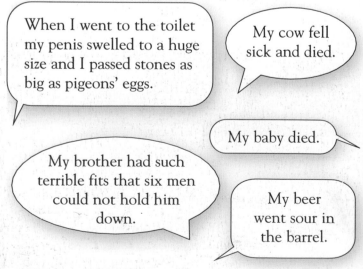

When I went to the toilet my penis swelled to a huge size and I passed stones as big as pigeons' eggs.

My cow fell sick and died.

My baby died.

My brother had such terrible fits that six men could not hold him down.

My beer went sour in the barrel.

1 Think about witch-marks and familiars. Why would it have been easy to claim that an innocent old woman was a witch?

2 Think about the things witches were accused of. How would we explain these things nowadays? Why did people in the sixteenth and seventeenth centuries blame witches?

3 Using your answers to these questions add more points to the list you began in Step 1.

# Two tests for witchcraft

## The first test

This is a picture from a seventeenth-century book on witchcraft. It shows the trial of Mary Sutton in 1612. Her hands have been tied and she is being lowered into the water. The rules of witchcraft trials said that if she floated she was a witch, and that if she sank she was innocent.

## The second test

Another test for witchcraft was to look for the witch-mark where familiars sucked blood. A large pin was stuck into the witch where the mark was. If she felt no pain and did not bleed then she was a witch.

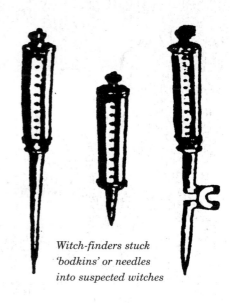

*The ducking of Mary Sutton.*
*A seventeenth-century illustration*

*Witch-finders stuck 'bodkins' or needles into suspected witches*

115

# Confessions

Even without being tortured many women confessed to being witches and were hanged.

## *The confession of Ursula Kemp*

In 1582, thirteen women from the village of St Osyth in Essex were accused of witchcraft. Details of the trial were recorded at the time. One of the accused women was Ursula Kemp who, it was claimed, had used the Black Art to kill several of her neighbours. Ursula's eight-year-old son gave evidence at the trial and this is what he said:

> My mother had four imps (familiars) at home – Tiffin, like a white lamb; Tilly, a little grey cat; Piggin, a black toad and Jack, a black cat. She fed them at times with milk and bread and at times they sucked blood from her body. My mother bewitched Johnson and his wife to death.

Later in the trial Ursula Kemp was questioned about her crimes by Lord Darcy, the judge. At first she refused to confess, but when Lord Darcy promised a light sentence, she burst out crying, fell on her knees and said:

> Yes I had the four imps my son has told of. Two of them, Tilly and Jack, were 'hees', whose job was to kill people. Two, Tiffin and Piggin were 'shes', who punished, made people lame and destroyed goods and cattle. I confess that I killed my brother's wife, and Grace Thurlow's child (I made it fall out of its cradle and break its neck). I bewitched the little babe of Annie Letherdall.

During the period of the witch-craze there were many women like Ursula Kemp who confessed to being witches.

# Village tensions

## *Elizabeth Crossley: Witch*

Henry Cockroft was a cloth-worker from Heptonstall in Yorkshire. In 1646, he told how Elizabeth Crossley, a poor woman in the village, came to his house begging for money. Elizabeth was not very pleased with the small amount Henry gave her, but she went away.

The next night Henry's one-year-old son began to have fits. Three months later he was dead. Henry accused Elizabeth Crossley of bewitching his child. At her trial, other people from Heptonstall reported that members of their families had also been bewitched by Crossley. Elizabeth Crossley was found guilty of witchcraft and hanged.

Historians have examined carefully the evidence from witchcraft trials like this and have found a lot of similarity between them.

## Four general findings from the trials

1 It was often richer people who accused women of being witches.

2 Nearly all the people accused of witchcraft were female, old and poor.

3 Often the problem began with a small quarrel between neighbours.

4 Witches were nearly always accused of causing harm to their neighbours rather than of worshipping the Devil.

**STEP 4**

From the sections called 'Two tests for witchcraft', 'Confessions' and 'Village tensions' (pages 115 to 117) add more points to the list you began in Step 1.

# Thinking your enquiry through

**So why did people in the sixteenth and seventeenth centuries believe in witches? You are now going to write an essay to answer the question.**

1 **Sorting the reasons**

You have a long list of reasons, but at the moment your ideas are in no particular order. You need to sort them out so that your essay will be clear.

Sort your reasons out under these headings:

<u>Lack of knowledge</u>, <u>Fear</u>, <u>Tension between rich and poor</u>, <u>The law</u>

Choose a better way to sort them out if you prefer.

2 **Starting the paragraphs**

Each group of reasons will form a paragraph in your essay. Here are some ways to start your paragraphs. You can use them in any order or make up your own paragraph-starters if you prefer:

- One of the most important reasons why people believed in witches in the sixteenth and seventeenth centuries was ...
- People also believed in witches because ...
- Lack of knowledge about how the world worked was another important reason why so many people believed in witches.
- Perhaps the main reason why people believed in witches was ...

Look back at the different sections in this enquiry to find details which support your ideas.

117

# 'Words new and unheard of'

## 14

## How did ideas change when great minds went to work?

At the start of the seventeenth century thousands of people believed in witchcraft and superstition. But some were beginning to take a very different approach to the world around them. Here are the words of an English doctor, called William Gilbert, written in 1600:

> The idea of science is almost a new thing. Therefore we sometimes use words new and unheard-of, so that hidden things, which have no name, may be plainly and fully published.

## Think

- Why did scientists have to find new words at this time?

- Scientists still have to invent new words. Think of some new, scientific words which we have only started to use in the twentieth century.

People like Gilbert were very **excited**. They believed that the human mind could unlock nature's secrets and explain the world using science instead of superstition. They often met to help each other and in 1662 a new scientific organisation was formed with the help of King Charles II. It was called the Royal Society.

## Your enquiry

This enquiry introduces you to four scientists who joined the Royal Society in its early days. They had such a great desire to explore the world of nature that they followed all sorts of ideas in all sorts of directions. But you will discover that they had some very important things in common.

# Changing ideas about building

## Sir Christopher Wren (1632–1732)

*A print of the Great Fire of London, made in 1666*

Early on Sunday, 2 September 1666, a bakery in Pudding Lane, London caught fire. A strong east wind fanned the flames. The fire spread. For the next three days flames raged through the narrow alleys and overhanging houses of London. The heat was so intense that the stones of St Paul's Church exploded and its lead roof melted like snow. By the time the fire had died away, the centre of one of Europe's biggest and most populated cities had been gutted.

A few days after the disaster, Sir Christopher Wren – who later became the President of the Royal Society – worked out a plan to rebuild the city. He followed the ideas of an Italian architect called Palladio. There were to be streets laid out in a careful pattern with wide avenues. There were to be 'piazzas' (from the Italian word for a square) with fountains and public gardens. He promised to build over fifty new churches and to replace the old St Paul's Church with a grand cathedral. This cathedral would be crowned not with a tower or a spire but with something new: something which Wren called a 'dome'.

## Think

- Which two words used by Wren would have been new to people in London?

119

Charles II had gathered a committee to decide how London should be rebuilt. When the committee members saw Wren's plans they were shocked. They wondered why his cathedral was not going to be like one of the great medieval churches with huge arches which pointed high into the sky and which made people think of heaven – the next world.

In fact, Wren was more interested in this world than the next. He had done all sorts of experiments with clocks, magnets and secret codes. He invented a pen which wrote two copies at a time. He improved suspension systems for coaches – and he experimented with the way domes helped to make the sound of human voices carry clearly through the air. Above all, he was a great **astronomer** and mathematician. He admired the way nature seemed to follow simple rules and patterns. He once said: 'True beauty comes from geometry'. Wren wanted to make London a place where simple columns, curves, angles and squares reminded people how orderly and beautiful their own world is.

In the end, Wren's plans for London were rejected. They were too ambitious and too expensive. But Wren was allowed to design the new St Paul's. It was finished in 1709 and still stands today. The artist's reconstruction on this page shows how Wren used simple shapes and angles to keep up the massive dome above the cathedral.

## Think

- Why did Wren admire nature?
- Which simple shapes from geometry can you see in the picture?

## STEP 1

**Make a factfile about Christopher Wren. Use the headings below. Add an illustration if you like.**

Name:

Born:

Died:

His achievements:

People who helped him:

New word(s) he introduced:

# Changing ideas about the body

## Robert Hooke (1635–1702)

Soon after the Royal Society was set up in 1662 its members decided that one of them should be **paid** to organise its work. The job went to Robert Hooke.

Hooke was soon doing experiments on all sorts of things: he studied light rays, planets, metal springs, fossils, earthquakes, underwater breathing equipment and how the human body worked. Here is his account of a rather gruesome experiment he did in 1664:

> The experiment was with a dog. I cut open its body and cut off all the ribs. Then, with a pair of bellows, I filled its lungs and allowed them to empty them again. The dog remained alive so long as I did this. My design was to study the nature of breathing, but I shall hardly wish to make any further trials of this kind because of the torture to the creature.

## Think

- Why did Hooke do this experiment?
- Why can we call Hooke a 'professional scientist'?

Hooke was trying to build on the work of another great English scientist, called William Harvey, who had died in 1657. Harvey was a doctor who had learnt a lot by studying in Italy. He had used scientific calculations and experiments to prove that blood must go around the human body, pumped by the heart. This was a very important new discovery.

*This painting shows William Harvey demonstrating to Charles I his theory of the circulation of the blood*

Hooke wanted to improve medicine. Doctors in the seventeenth century had made little progress since the Middle Ages. When a terrible outbreak of plague hit London in 1665 over 80,000 people died in just a few months. No one knew what caused plague: some said the air was infected with poison. We now know that it is caused by germs which are spread by fleas living on rats.

In the seventeenth century no one knew that germs existed. But the work of men like Robert Hooke soon changed that. Hooke made a very powerful microscope. A Dutch spectacle maker had invented the first simple microscope in 1609 but Hooke's was much more powerful.

In 1665, Hooke wrote a book which contained his own detailed drawings of objects seen through his microscope. He was astonished to see that plants were made up of small sections. He decided to call these 'cells'. It was only later that scientists found out how important cells are in the life of plants and humans.

## Think

● What new word did Hooke invent?

In 1683, a Dutchman called van Leeuwenhoek saw something even more amazing through his own microscope. He saw tiny living creatures (which we call germs). It was to be another two hundred years before other scientists realised that these could cause diseases like the plague. Without microscopes such as Hooke's it is hard to imagine how scientific discoveries about medicine could have happened.

## Think

● According to people in 1665 what caused the plague?

● Why did no one know about germs in 1665?

**STEP 2**

**Write a factfile about Robert Hooke like the one shown in Step 1.**

# Changing ideas about space

## Sir Isaac Newton (1642–1727)

Most people agree that the greatest scientist of the time was Sir Isaac Newton. Newton was Professor of Mathematics at Cambridge University. Like Hooke and Wren, he could hardly stop himself from studying the stars, light rays, liquids and many other wonders of the world. In 1687 he wrote many of his most important ideas in a book called 'Principia'. He explained that the universe worked according to a few important rules and ran like a clock which God had made. 'Principia' was to be the most important book about science for over two hundred years.

One of Newton's most important discoveries was about the force which holds planets together in space. He decided to call the force 'gravity'.

He had been trying to work out why something like an apple fell to earth, but other things, like the moon did not. He wanted to explain it. He knew that planets move around the sun. He showed that the planets are kept in place by two forces – their own speed and the gravity of the sun.

Newton's ideas were not the first. There had been many new discoveries since the Middle Ages and Newton would have read about them and built upon them. In the Middle Ages the Church taught people that the earth was the centre of the universe and that all other planets and stars travelled around it. The Bible seemed to say that this was right.

In 1543, Nicholas Copernicus, a Polish astronomer, suggested that the Bible was wrong and that all planets travelled around the sun – but he could not prove this. The trouble was that he had to rely on the power of his own eyes to see what was going on in space.

## Think

- What word did Newton use for his discovery about planets?

- How did he let others know of his discoveries?

*A picture of the Solar System with the sun at the centre*

Then, in 1610, an Italian called Galileo built a telescope that magnified everything 32 times. Using this instrument he was able to prove that Copernicus was right – and to make many other important discoveries.

Newton had read about the ideas of Copernicus and Galileo. He made a powerful telescope of his own and did some very complicated **calculations** about the movements of the planets. These led to his ideas about gravity. Modern scientists still use Newton's calculations to work out how to put satellites in space!

## STEP 3

Make a factfile about Isaac Newton like the one shown in Step 1.

## Think

● What is the difference between a microscope and a telescope?

● What new understanding did Newton's ideas add to Galileo's ideas?

# Changing ideas about energy

## Thomas Savery (1650–1715)

Our fourth scientist did not just want to understand the forces of nature, he wanted to use them.

Up to the year 1700, people worked using the power of their own muscles. If more power was needed they used animals to pull wagons and ploughs. If a fast-flowing stream was nearby they could use it to drive a waterwheel.

The power of the wind could also be used. The wind turned the sails of a windmill which could then drive machinery inside. The power was usually used for grinding corn but in areas where coal was found, it was often used to drain water from mines. On calm days the windmills could not work and mines would get flooded.

In 1698, an English scientist invented a machine which did not depend on the weather to make power. His name was Thomas Savery. He knew that a Royal Society scientist from Ireland, called Robert Boyle, had been experimenting with vacuums. Savery learned that a Frenchman, called Papin, had been trying to use vacuums to make pumps.

Savery did some calculations and experiments of his own and came up with his 'Engine for raising water by fire'. Fire heated water to make steam. The steam made a vacuum which sucked water through a long pipe that reached down into the mine.

Savery used a new word to describe the power of his machine. He guessed how many horses would be needed to do its work and called it a two 'horsepower' engine. After Savery died, the power of steam engines improved and changed the whole history of the world. But that is another story!

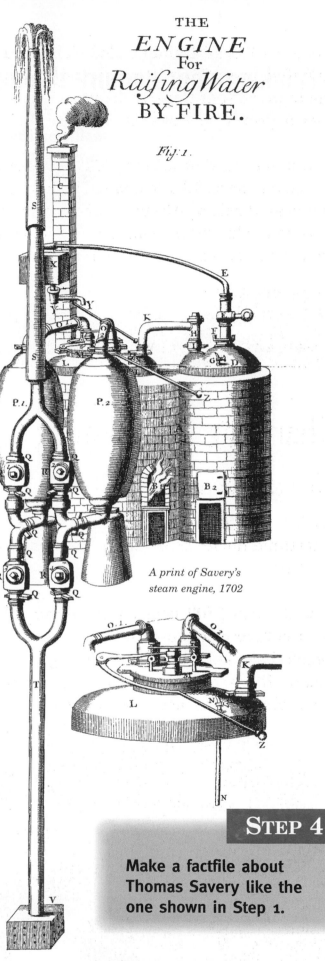

A print of Savery's steam engine, 1702

## Think

- What new word did Savery introduce?

- Why was his engine better than a windmill or watermill?

## STEP 4

**Make a factfile about Thomas Savery like the one shown in Step 1.**

# Thinking your enquiry through

Copy the chart below and fill it in. The first box is about Wren and mathematical calculations. If you know Wren used mathematical calculations in his work, put a tick in that box. If you think he did not use them, put a cross in the box. Work through all the boxes. You can check that you are right by using your factfile or the information in this chapter.

|  | Wren | Hooke | Newton | Savery |
|---|---|---|---|---|
| 'I used mathematical calculations in my work' |  |  |  |  |
| 'I was helped by the Royal Society' |  |  |  |  |
| 'I used microscopes or telescopes' |  |  |  |  |
| 'I got ideas from other countries in Europe' |  |  |  |  |
| 'I was really excited by all sorts of scientific work' |  |  |  |  |
| 'I had to introduce a new word' |  |  |  |  |

# Glossary

**almshouses**    Houses built by rich people for poor people to live in

**Armada**    A powerful fleet of ships

**astronomer**    A person who studies the stars

**baptism**    A church service where a person is welcomed as a new member of the church (This is often done to babies)

**beadle**    A man who has to find and arrest any vagrants

**bear baiting**    A sport where a bear was chained to a post while dogs attacked it

**borderer**    People who live in the borders between England and Scotland

**burgess**    A powerful man who helped to run a city

**calculation**    Doing sums

**Cavalier**    A nickname for supporters of the king in the English Civil War

**church-warden**    A person who helps a vicar to run a parish (Not a priest)

**civil war**    A war between people who belong to the same country

**clan**    A group of families

**colonies**    Lands which have been taken over by settlers from another country

**colonist**    A person who moves from one country to take land in another

**Common-wealth**    A name given to Britain from 1649 to 1660 when it had no king

**communion**    An important Protestant church service

**conclusion**    The end or a final decision about something

**corrupt**    Unfair, cheating or bad behaviour

**court**    Either the king or queen's household or a place where people are put on trial

**culture**    A way of life

**cutpurse**    A pickpocket

**execute**    To put someone to death

**exiled**    Sent away to live in another place

**gaol**    Prison

**gentry**    Rich people who had a lot of power in their county

**house of correction**    A place where poor people were kept and made to work

**illegitimate**    Someone whose parents were not married to each other

**inhabitant**    Someone who lives in a place

**inherit**    To take something over (e.g. the throne) when someone dies

**interpretation**    A person's point of view or opinion about something

**inventories**    Lists of things which a person owned

**Justice of the Peace (JP)**    Someone who has to keep law and order in the parishes

**Lord Lieutenant**    A lord who has to keep law and order in a county

**lower sort**    Servants or labourers

**marches**    The land around a border, e.g. between England and Scotland

**martyr**    A person who has died for something that they believe in

**Mass**    An important Roman Catholic church service

| | |
|---|---|
| **mayor** | The person who is in charge of a town |
| **medieval** | From the Middle Ages |
| **merchants** | Traders |
| **middling sort** | Fairly rich farmers or traders |
| **ministers** | Servants of the king (politicians) or servants of God (vicars) |
| **monarch** | A king or queen |
| **monastery** | A place where monks or nuns live and worship |
| **parish** | The area served by a church (The whole country was divided into thousands of parishes) |
| **persecute** | To attack or pick on a person in a cruel way |
| **plague** | A serious disease which spreads quickly |
| **Pope** | The powerful leader of the Roman Catholic Church |
| **population** | The total number of people living in a place |
| **Presbyterian** | A system where people choose their own church leaders |
| **Privy Council** | A group of people who advise the king or queen |
| **propaganda** | One-sided views |
| **Protestant** | A Christian who does not like the old Roman Catholic Church and protests against it |
| **Puritan** | A very strict Protestant who wants people to obey the bible and to live pure, holy lives |
| **rate** | A tax paid by people to look after the poor in their area |
| **Reformation** | The time in the sixteenth century when many Protestant churches started |
| **register** | A record book |
| **republic** | A way of running a country without a king or queen |
| **rogues** | Beggars who try to trick people out of their money |
| **Roman Catholic** | A Christian who belongs to one of the oldest branches of the church, led by the Pope |
| **Roundhead** | A nickname for supporters of Parliament in the English Civil War |
| **settler** | A person who moves from one country to live in another |
| **society** | A group of people who live or work together |
| **sources** | Objects (e.g. books, diaries, paintings) which historians use to find out about the past |
| **superstitious** | Believing in powers which seem magical |
| **traitor** | Someone who plots against a monarch or their own country |
| **treason** | The crime of plotting against your own king or country |
| **tyrant** | Someone with great power who rules in a cruel way |
| **vagabond, vagrant** | A wandering beggar |
| **vestments** | Special clothes worn by priests |
| **warden** | A person who has to control an area of land |
| **witch-craze** | A time when many people were scared of witchcraft and put thousands of 'witches' to death |
| **workhouse** | See 'house of correction' |
| **yeoman** | A farmer who owned or rented some land |

THIS WALKER BOOK BELONGS TO:

_____

_____

_____

_____

# The Nursery Collection

## Shirley Hughes

WALKER BOOKS

AND SUBSIDIARIES

LONDON · BOSTON · SYDNEY

First published individually as
*Bathwater's Hot, When We Went to the Park,*
*Noisy* (1985), and *Colours*
and *All Shapes and Sizes* (1986)
by Walker Books Ltd
87 Vauxhall Walk, London SE11 5HJ

This edition published 1997

8 10 9 7

© 1985, 1986 Shirley Hughes

This book has been typeset in Sabon

Printed in China

All rights reserved

British Library Cataloguing in Publication Data:
a catalogue record for this book is
available from the British Library

ISBN 0-7445-4378-9

www.walkerbooks.co.uk

# Contents

# Bathwater's Hot

Bathwater's hot,

Seawater's cold;

Ginger's kittens are *very* young,

But Buster's getting old.

Some things
you can
throw away,

Some are nice to keep;

Here's someone
who is wide awake...

Shhh, he's fast asleep!

Some things are hard as stone,

Some are soft as cloud;

Whisper very

quietly,

Shout

OUT LOUD!

It's fun to run
very fast,

Or to be slow;

The red light
says "stop",

And the green
light says "go".

It's kind to be helpful,

Unkind to tease;

Rather rude to push and grab,

Polite to say "please".

Night-time is dark,   Daytime is light;

18

The sun says
"good morning",

And the moon
says "good night".

Good night!

19

# When We Went
# to the Park

When Grandpa
and I put on our
coats and went
to the park...

We saw one black
cat sitting on a wall,

Two big
girls licking
ice-creams,

Three ladies chatting on a bench,

Four babies in buggies,

Five children playing in the sandpit,

Six runners running,

Seven dogs chasing one another,

Eight boys kicking a ball,

Nine ducks swimming on the pond,

25

Ten birds swooping
in the sky,

And so many leaves that
I couldn't count them all.

On the way back we saw
the black cat again.

Then we went home for tea.

# Colours

Baby blues, navy blues,
Blue socks, blue shoes;

Blue plate, blue mug,
Blue flowers in a blue jug;

And fluffy white clouds floating by
In a great big beautiful bright blue sky.

Syrup dripping from a spoon,
Buttercups, a harvest moon;
Sun like honey on the floor,
Warm as the steps by our back door.

Scarlet leaves, bright berries,

Rosy apples, dark cherries;

And when the winter's day is done,

A fiery sky, a big red sun.

Tangerines and apricots,
Orange flowers in orange pots;
Orange glow on an orange mat,
Marmalade toast and a marmalade cat.

Berries in the bramble patch,
Pick them (but mind the thorns don't scratch)!
Purple blossom, pale and dark,
Spreading with springtime in the park.

Green lettuce, green peas,
Green shade from green trees;
And grass as far as you can see,
Like green waves in a green sea.

Shiny boots, a witch's hat,
Black cloak, black cat;
Black crows cawing high,
Winter trees against the sky.

Thistledown like white fluff,
Dandelion clocks to puff;
White snowflakes whirling down,
Covering gardens, roofs and town.

# All Shapes and Sizes

Boxes have flat sides,
Balls are round;

High is
far up in
the sky,

Low is
near the
ground.

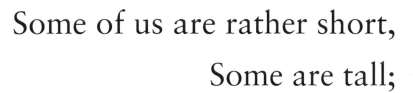

Some of us are rather short,
Some are tall;

Some pets are large, some are small.

Our cat's very fat,    Next door's is thin;

Big Teddy's out,    Little Teddy's in.

Squeeze through narrow spaces,

Run through wide;

Climb up the ladder,

Slip down the slide.

Get behind to push,

Get in front
to pull;

This
jar's
empty,

Now
it's
full.

48

Hats can be
many sizes,

So can feet;

Children of all ages playing in the street.

I can stand up
very straight,

Or I can
bend.

Here's a beginning,

And this is the end!

# Noisy

Noisy noises! Pan lids clashing,

Dog barking, plate smashing;

Telephone ringing, baby bawling,
Midnight cats
cat-a-wauling.

Door slamming,
Aeroplane zooming,

Vacuum cleaner
Vroom-vroom-
vrooming;

And if I dance
and sing a tune,
Baby joins in
with a saucepan
and spoon.

Gentle noises: dry leaves swishing,
Falling rain, splashing, splishing;

Rustling trees, hardly stirring,
Lazy cat softly purring.

Story's over,
Bedtime's come,

Crooning baby
Sucks his thumb;

60

All quiet, not a peep –
Everyone is fast asleep.